P9-AGU-691

Reader Reviews

Loved this book! It is the best book I've read on male relationships. It's about changing ourselves and influencing others by nature of that change. I took all the training in the early days of *Promise Keepers* in order to be a trainer for *Honorbound* which is the men's ministries of the denomination I serve. I've got all the books, and then some. And this book is incredible stuff! I detest the thought of relating any quote by Jack Nicholson in life or a film as an application to my own soul. But his quote in "As Good as it Gets," says it all for me. I paraphrase, "This book 'makes me want to be a better man.'"

Dr. Mike Johnson
Assembly of God Pastor

The book provides a compelling and thoughtful outline for improving men's relationships with one another. I really enjoy how the book (literally) emerges from a dialogue between the authors. There is also a distinctively open, even confessional quality in the book that is very genuine and poignant. Both authors openly share from their own foibles and difficult experiences. I also appreciate how the book mixes the paradigmatic qualities of Christlike friendship with the cautionary tales provided by the lives of less salutary characters (you specifically mention Saddam Hussein and Bernie Madoff, while paying sustained attention to Judas). Lastly, the discussion questions make this book very useful for men's groups in churches. Bravo!

Dr. John Bartkowski
Professor of Sociology
Specializing in Faith-Based Organizations
University of Texas at San Antonio

I was so blessed and challenged by every page of this book. The two high performance friends and authors have done an incredible job expressing principles of friendship in a sensitive, compassionate, straight-forward, transparent and effective way. They have done a great job of infusing Scriptural truth with practical application and experience to make the subject of the book come alive. It is a must read for every man desiring to build friendships to a high performance level. I know I have been challenged to be a better friend. This is an incredible and critically important book at a critical time.

Dr. Bill Faulkner
Southern Baptist Association Missions Executive

This is a book of respect—how to respect yourself and how to respect your friends. Men will read a chapter and then be motivated to join a small group to discuss the book. I can see this book being a great help to college and university students—who in many cases do not have any significant friendships. Thanks for your fine work.

Chuck Schwaninger
Cru Staff Member

A powerful book. The stories the authors share in each chapter of their personal experiences make the book come alive. I could relate to many of them myself. It is a book that will change the lives of those who read it. We men need to hear this message.

Reuel Nygaard
Author and Speaker

A must read for men, especially young ones. The sooner men realize the importance of developing deep friendships, the better and longer they will be served by them! The authors do a great job of building the reasons why men of all ages need good friendships. I couldn't help but feel convicted myself while reading and I don't particularly feel that I lack Biblical friendships.

Mike Hancock
Family Pastor

I love the way stories are used in this book, especially the way they go back and forth between the authors to make compelling points about friendship. Communicating by stories is powerful and is the way so many of us, including me, are wired to learn. I especially liked the Intimacy chapter. It is important talk about the sexual areas of our lives (men get that confused with intimacy) and I loved how the authors told the story about how they each had unwanted advances from other males. This is such a difficult area for guys to talk about and your honesty will give them freedom to share their own stories.

Kevin Sharpe
Converge (General Conference Baptist) Lead Pastor

I am so moved by all of this book. One specific story in particular reminds me of a time in 1971 when my father was at home dying of cancer. We didn't face "dying" quite like we often do these days so he lay in bed watching TV without a way to share his utmost fear. Only during his last month on earth did I hear him behind closed doors cry out to my mother in anguish "I'm not afraid to die—Yes I AM Afraid to die." I will never forget those words. I remember that his BEST friend NEVER came to see him during his illness—not one time. Men do need to learn how to be better friends.

Gaydee Gardner
Business Owner

This book will make men stronger with each other and with Christ. Churches will be better because better men are in the church because of the book. The church will not know what to do with so many good men. The book can serve as a mentor for men. The book underlines the need for sociology so the church understands men in its culture.

Dr. Dale Sharp
Evangelical Free Pastor

A timely and well written book. I found the "teach by personal experience" style very credible and easy to read and understand. The conversational narrative draws one *in* to feel a part what is going on. The topics were well chosen and what man would not want to be more Christlike?

Gary Buckmiller
Retired Business Executive and Seminary Board Member

This book is great. I thoroughly enjoyed it. After reading it, I'm all the more grateful for the relationships I have and am more challenged to continue to build friendships. The material in the book is so helpful, I asked and received permission to use material from the book in my blog.

Ray Burwick, Ed.D.

This is a wonderful book and very well done on an unusual and difficult topic. I thoroughly enjoyed it. The authors are spot on that men do not make very many friendships. It is very interesting how the authors related the attributes/characteristics of a high performance friendship to Christlike characteristics from the Gospel and Proverbs. Even as someone who doesn't read the Bible regularly, the Bible references were compelling. Reading the book has made me more thoughtful of my relationships with others. My last general observation is that the entire book on how to achieve high performance friendship is applicable and can easily be used and enjoyed by non-Christians. They may enjoy the fact that these attributes are the same as the Christian's Jesus Christ, but they could work to achieve them and value them just as much if not more than Christians.

Ron Lappi
Retired City Financial Director

This book is excellent and such a blessing. We used it in a men's group and were amazed at how the principles in the book are so true within various levels among us.

Marvin Harms
Educator and Church Board Chairman

GREAT stuff. I will use it as a very valuable tool in coaching, mentoring and discipleship. I was personally challenged and blessed by the read. Loved the format. The strength of the content came from the anecdotal experiences shared. Great application. I appreciated, as well, the great way the authors used Jesus as a role model both from his lifestyle—the observations on how he treated his friends—and the content of his teaching. It all seemed to *fit* together.

Sam Owen
Veteran Missionary

The personal stories shared by the authors are very powerful and helpful.

Dr. Rick Penner
Director, CARES of Canada

The statement in the introduction, "It is sad that most men live activity-driven lives where urgency drives out importance" really touched me. So true.

Duane Ehler
Mortgage Business Executive

Achieving High Performance Friendship

A Book For Men

John Vawter
&
James Wetherbe

Mead Publishing

Texas USA

Achieving
High Performance
Friendship

A Book For Men

Copyright © 2012, MEAD PUBLISHING

PRINTED AND BOUND BY WORZALLA PUBLISHING CO.
STEVENS POINT, WISCONSIN USA

All rights reserved. No part of this book may be reproduced or transmitted in any form or by any electronic or mechanical means without permission in writing from the publisher, except by a reviewer, who may quote brief passages in a review.

ISBN: 978-1-883096-06-9

Published by Mead Publishing
P.O. Box 6890
Lubbock, TX 79493-6890
U.S.A.

Mead Publishing books are available at special discounts for bulk purchases by corporations, institutions and other organizations.

For more information, please contact Mead Publishing at:

Phone: (713) 553-4020
          (281) 610-4064
Email: meadpublishing@att.net
Website: http://www.meadpublications.com

Dedication

To my wife Susan
the embodiment of Christ's "grace and truth"
and
the finest minister in my life.
John

To my wife Brynn
who knows all my failings and weaknesses
but
loves me nonetheless and encourages my faith in God.
Jim

About the Authors

Dr. John Vawter spent 10 years on the staff of Cru (formerly Campus Crusade for Christ) in both England and Northwestern USA as Area Director. For eighteen years, he pastored Wayzata Evangelical Free Church in the suburbs of Minneapolis and Bethany Community Church in Tempe, AZ. He was the president of Phoenix Seminary in Phoenix and Western Seminary in Portland, OR. He has taught doctoral courses in six different seminaries and spoken in seventeen countries.

His two previous books are **Uncommon Graces: Christ-Like Responses to A Hostile World,** which was nominated for the Gold Medallion Award, and **Hit by a Ton of Bricks: You're Not Alone When Your Child's on Drugs**. The latter book grew out of the ministry his wife and he founded, called *You're Not Alone, Inc.,* a non-profit ministry aimed at helping parents who discover their children are abusing alcohol and other drugs. The website, *www.notalone.org,* is visited by thousands of people every year. His daily radio program is heard on over 418 stations in the United States.

Dr. James Wetherbe is a professor, author and consultant in Management of Information Technology. He has spent over forty years in academia and industry, serving on the faculty of the University of Houston, University of Minnesota, University of Memphis and Texas Tech University. Author of over thirty books, he has lectured worldwide on leadership, communication and information technology.

He was the first recipient of the Management Information Systems Quarterly Distinguished Scholar Award, was ranked by *Information Week* as one of the top dozen information technology consultants and speakers and is ranked among the top twenty most influential researchers in his field. His book about FedEx, **The World on Time**, was ranked as one of the top thirty business books of 1997, by *Executive Book Summaries. Computing Newsletter* ranked his book, **Systems Analysis and Design**, as the best textbook on the topic. Previous work in spiritual authoring includes **Faith Logic: Getting Online with God**, aimed at the strong-willed spiritually-challenged who require a more logical, reasoned approach to arrive at faith in God.

Table of Contents

Preface		xiv
	Introduction	1
1	Choose Friends Wisely	17
2	Humility and Honesty	39
3	Respect	61
4	Intimacy	77
5	Support	95
6	Trust and Teach	115
7	Love and Loyalty	131
8	Independence and Inner Compass	149
9	Kindness	171
10	Encouragement and Eternal Values	189
	Summary and Conclusions	207
	Epilogue	213
	References	219
	Index of Bible Verses	221

Preface

Men commonly experience life without deep meaningful friendships. As explained in the introduction, the aim of this book is to help men achieve high performance friendship. We consider high performance friendship to include respect, selflessness, intimacy, trust, support and heartfelt constructive criticism void of jealousy and disparagement. Striving to develop high performance friendships is a powerful enhancement to our lives.

We have found and believe that men can achieve high performance friendship by applying the over-arching lessons learned in this book, which draw from the way Christ treated His male friends during His human experience. The principles we share in the book have helped us in our own friendships and we hope you find them helpful in yours.

This book is our gift to you—we take no royalties for this book. John donates his royalties to the non-profit ministry, *You're Not Alone, Inc., www.notalone.org*, which provides help for parents who discover their children are on drugs. His book, **Hit by a Ton of Bricks: You're Not Alone When Your Child's on Drugs**, grew out of this ministry. Jim donates his royalties through his church to scholarships for worthy students attending Texas Tech University.

If you are not yet a person of faith, we hope that if you know we had no financial motivation for writing this book, you might be more open to the authenticity with which we share our thoughts and experiences. Though the title of the book is **Achieving High Performance Friendship**, we believe that is best accomplished in concert with *achieving high performance faith*.

We had the benefit of numerous and wonderful colleagues and friends to review the text and make many helpful suggestions. The goal was to make the book straightforward, practical and accessible. We offer special thanks to: Dr. John Aker, Dr. Dennis

Baker, Dr. John Bartkowski, Gene Bourland, Craig Bourne, Gary Buckmiller, Bob Buday, Dr. Bill Faulkner, Dr. David Fisher, Gaydee Gardner, Doug Goostree, Tom Hagen, Mike Hancock, Marvin Harms, David Harowitz, Dr. James Hoffman, James Holder, Dr. Brian Janz, Dr. Mike Johnson, Cort Jones, Dianne Gobel Meyer, Grace Noyes, Reuel Nygaard, Jamin Pillars, Dr. Rick Penner, Kevin Sharpe, Lynnda Speer, Dr. Ken Sylvester, Dr. Michael Vawter, Stephanie Vawter, Jim Vieburg, Thom Vines, Bob Walker, Michael Westphal, Bond Wetherbe and Faye Wetherbe.

One reviewer, Craig Bourne, provided much more than just a review. At the beginning of the project, Craig, an acquaintance of John, offered to review the manuscript. More than a review, we had the benefit of professional quality editing, which Craig, having spent time as both a technical writer and an English teacher, was able to provide. Craig's volunteer contributions revealed to us a generous and talented colleague who became a friend through our collaboration.

Most importantly we want to thank our wives, Susan (John's) and Brynn (Jim's), for putting up with the persistent interruption of home life that is associated with authoring. Those moments when an author's thoughts drift away from a conversation and start *authoring* take great tolerance and patience from a spouse—as do those times when an author gets up in the middle of the night to capture a thought that might be gone by morning. We also, in our stream of consciousness, were perpetually bouncing ideas off them—including in the middle of the night. Our wives offered great guidance, as they were typically the first eyes to read an original draft of a new section of text. It is easier to take criticism and suggestions from someone who loves and puts up with you. We both are truly blessed.

As we acknowledge the efforts of all who have contributed, we also assume full responsibility for any inadequacies or discrepancies in the text.

John Vawter
James Wetherbe

Introduction

The worst solitude is to be destitute of sincere friendship
~ Francis Bacon

This is a book for male friends, collaboratively written by two long-term friends—John is a minister and Jim is a professor. Our friendship has grown and matured over the past 30 years and both of us are authors, international consultants and speakers. Our main credential for undertaking this topic is that we have each enjoyed multiple decades with many friends, some of whom encouraged us to consider this project. John did that in the form of a sermon series and speaking at conferences for men, but up until this point, he had never taken the time to write on the subject.

The two of us began to share ideas about friendship, and once we realized this would be a worthy project, we decided to make the time for it. While we had both authored books separately, we had never worked on one together. We were willing, however, to jeopardize it all with the risky venture of co-authoring a book, which we are told is a true test of friendship survival!

Why are we limiting our focus to just men? Simply because, though male friendships are romanticized in tales of bravery, it is rare that men have intimate, open relationships with those whom they consider their friends. Whereas women very naturally share themselves with friends through acceptance and self-revealing conversations, men shy away from intimacy, as pointed out in **Friendship Among Men** (Fasteau, 1991), The *McGill Report on Male Intimacy* (1985) and **Men and Friendship** (Miller, 1983).

Or put in a more humorous way:

Friends are generally of the same sex, for when men and women agree, it is only in the conclusions; their reasons are always different.

~ *George Santayana*

Before we go any further, we want to make a clear caveat: though this is a book about male friendship, both of us consider our wives to be our absolute best friends. John's wife, Susan, and Jim's wife, Brynn, are soul-mates with whom we share our lives, our love and all that we are.

While we have been working on the book, John's older brother, Dr. Michael Vawter, has been on his sixth two-week fishing trip to New Zealand with his college friend of over 50 years, Dar Isensee. Due to airline ticket problems, Mike and Dar were unable to fly home on the same flight. Mike told John that Dar said, "After two weeks together we will be sick of each other anyway." As men we understand the comment Dar made to Mike but we can honestly say we would not be tired of our wives after a two-week trip to New Zealand...or anywhere else. We know of no greater compliment to give our wives.

Years ago, we were challenged by David W. Smith's book, **The Friendless American Male** (1983), which sadly pointed out how most American males go through life in a lonely, friendless state, lacking close connection and intimacy with male friends. We find Smith's assessment to ring true for many men with whom we come into contact in our professional and personal lives. These men have acquaintances, but they do not have friends. They do a lot of shop talk, whether they are in business or ministry, but they rarely seem to dig into one another's lives and they don't allow others to dig into their lives. Tennis, golf, or fishing buddies are as deep as relationships go. They share activities, yes, but share feelings? No. Very briefly, we often see *friend* used when we should be using *acquaintance* or *pal*. Acquaintances know each other enough to say hello—pals do things together, but they do not delve into one another's lives.

Indeed, as we told friends that we were working together on this book, a number of them confessed immediately that they have very few friends. There are others who have many good friends. This led us to question, "Why do some men cultivate meaningful friendships, while others do not?" or "How can men who have avoided meaningful friendships or do not know how to have meaningful friendships chart a new course and reap the benefits such relationships can provide?" Answering these questions is the aim of this book.

The book is for men of all ages. For young men, the sooner they can develop meaningful friendships, the longer they will have the wonderful benefit of them. It is so meaningful to have friends with whom to share reflections on our lives as the years go by. For older men, the wisdom of having deep friendships becomes even more significant, for a lonely void exists in their lives without men who can share thoughtful conversations.

Without friends, there doesn't seem to be much self-reflection or introspection for many men. They rush from activity to activity but they do not look inside themselves. In the high-tech knowledge economy in which we live, much time is required just to keep up with our daily work demands. There are so many disruptions and distractions in our daily lives that time for sharing thoughts and feelings with friends can become a fatality.

Social media, e.g., *Facebook,* has become a high-tech dynamic of the friendship landscape. We can *friend* someone on *Facebook*, which in many cases cheapens the construct of friendship, as people often barely know and may not even recall those to whom they grant friendship status. While social media has helped us connect to others in incredible ways, it can also be a detriment to intimate friendships. In fact, it probably leads more people to have more superficial acquaintances than anything else. How can we possibly build friendships by writing short sentences on a wall where everyone else can read them? Who would share their most intimate thoughts and concerns in that manner?

Unfortunately, too many people are beginning to consider social media relationships with strangers a surrogate for deep friendships.

The Superficial Support Groups

Here is a story that is all too common and told to us by a man, "Bill," for whom we have great respect. He joined a number of men he knew in a professional support group that was intended to develop intimacy among them by discussing both personal and professional issues of importance. However, because of the typical avoidance of substantive personal issues, they soon lost the intended purpose of the group, and little true personal sharing took place.

Nonetheless, a number of the men saw a glaring inconsistency in the life of one of the other members, "Frank." Frank was constantly talking about himself, drawing attention to himself, and was obviously suffering from a deep insecurity that he masked through high profile activity and success in his profession. Though other men in the group voiced concern about the behavior among themselves, no one was willing to approach Frank in a constructive and helpful manner. As a friend, Bill wanted to take the lead and reach out to help—his heart was coming from a place of responsible friendship.

Bill reasoned that the best way to talk to Frank about what he saw was to go golfing together where he could gently raise the issue privately rather than in the group. On the way to the course, Frank said, "I am really tired emotionally today. I hope we do not have to discuss anything of importance." So Bill never raised the subject.

Bill then invited Frank out for lunch but he got stiff-armed again. He realized that Frank was frenetically busy with activities but he was not willing to look into his own soul. He was not interested in deep, meaningful discussions that come from a quality friendship. Rather, he created barriers to avoid it. Bill later realized that none of the men were willing to discuss this personal issue with Frank; the group had become a place to talk shop.

As stated earlier, this is an all too common phenomenon. We have seen groups where members had other inconsistencies in their lives: alcohol abuse, gambling abuse, mistreatment of their children, adultery, pornography, vulgar language, talking disrespectfully about their wives, talking disrespectfully about women in a sexual manner, etc. As was the case with Frank above, members of the groups, though willing to discuss the problem within the group, were unwilling to follow Jesus' instructions to privately talk to our brother if he is caught in a sin. If he refuses to listen, go with a witness. If he refuses again, he is to be brought before the church. Of course, the men's group is not a church but Christ's principles still apply.

In Bill's case, the group was not willing to work together to help Frank understand his need for helpful suggestions on how to improve.

When men play their cards close to the vest, there is little opportunity for the type of intimacy and growth that is possible through heartfelt friendship. It is sad that most men live activity-driven lives where urgency drives out importance.

John knows many ministers who study the Bible to learn what other people are doing wrong and how those people should improve when preparing and delivering great sermons. Rarely, as they study the Bible for those sermons, do they seem as interested in letting God speak to them about the areas where they themselves need to grow.

Someone has said the sin of young men is passion, the sin of middle age men is pride and the sin of senior age men is prejudice. Thus, it makes no difference what our age is—we are tempted to sin, to think too highly of ourselves and to be less than Christ wants us to be. This is why we need men to tell us the truth—good or bad—and to help us grow. Wes Yoder writes in **Bond of Brothers** (Zondervan, 2010) that it is hard for men to be truthful; indeed, he has watched men sit in accountability groups and not tell the truth. But Jesus was full of grace and truth.

As we reflected on our own friendship, one that has included the closeness and openness that many men fear, we realized we could not take any particular credit for our good fortune. We concluded that we probably had many lifetime friends between us, primarily because we loved and needed friends. We had no particular skill set other than that we both were brought up with the "do unto others as you would have them do unto you" value system that comes from a Christian upbringing. Or as Emerson said, "The only way to have a friend is to be one." We both wanted friends, so we have tried to be worthy of friendship.

The Reality for Men

One of John's very good friends seems to know people and is known by people wherever he goes. He became very ill almost overnight. What initially seemed to be a fast-growing and potentially fatal tumor turned out to be a very serious but treatable and curable strange infection. He was ill for some time but is now fully recovered. The first time John saw him after he was well, his friend said, "I lay in the hospital bed and did some very deep thinking. I realized that I have lots of acquaintances but very few friends—maybe 2-3 friends. I hope you are one of them."

John repeated this story to a woman who is a dear friend of John and his wife Susan. Her husband has retired from a company that he built and owned—a company that is worth over a billion dollars. Her response was, "My husband does not have any friends. He has a couple of friends that are committed to him but he is committed to no one. Thus, at 78 he is a lonely old man."

6

Later, John asked her to read this chapter and make comments on it. When she saw the quote by Bacon used above—"The worst solitude is to be destitute of sincere friendship," she called John and exclaimed, "This is exactly what my husband is experiencing. He is absolutely alone." Imagine…all that financial success, a 300 foot long yacht and absolutely alone. It seems that no matter where we turn, men reveal that they do not have many, if any, friends.

In today's culture adulthood is often postponed for young men, tending to adversely affect developing relationships. Young men may take their time casually getting through college, hanging out, partying, watching TV, playing with tech toys and postponing starting a family. Kimmel, in his book, **Guyland** (2008), points out that today the average young man is evolving through a buddy culture, unfazed by the demands of parents, girlfriends, jobs, children and the nuisances of adult life. This arrested launch into adulthood inhibits maturity. It comes with less-than-useful attitudes and self-images carried into adulthood, with troubling implications for adult relationships.

A few years ago, John attended a fraternity reunion in Palo Alto before the Stanford/Oregon game. The Oregon team had asked John to be the chapel speaker. He took along two fraternity brothers—Dave and Rick. He told the players he had nothing to say about football but wanted to talk about friendship…and then pointed to Dave and Rick and said, "We are 62 years old and have been friends since we were 18 and met at the University of Oregon. When you are our age, I hope you have such good friends." That got the players' attention immediately in a profound manner. It was readily apparent that most of the young men in the room had never considered that they were surrounded by teammates that could be close friends forty years from then.

A troubling symptomatic phenomenon among males of all ages is that male suicides significantly exceed those of females. Though factors such as age, unemployment and chronic illness contribute to the higher rate of male suicides, social isolation is a major factor that compounds all others. According to *Netdoctor*, there is an increasing rate of suicide among young men, the majority of whom don't even ask for help before their deaths. And among senior citizens, Caucasian men are at the greatest risk, being six times more likely to commit suicide than any other demographic group.

In Search of Real Solutions

Rather than spending a lot of time trying to figure out why this has become such a pervasive phenomenon in our country, it seems more relevant to look to the future to define what genuine friendship is and to build a plan for men to follow in regard to friendships.

When a man was told we were working on this project, he blurted out, "Male friendships are the most impossible thing in the world. What does it take to maintain them?" Another man in an adult church class desperately complained, "We meet every week but I don't even have the phone number of a single man in this group." John was consulting at a church where the board met once a month. During a meeting, he heard two men who had served together for three years (that would be a minimum of 36 meetings during their tenure) ask each other what they did for their occupations.

It seems that many men have acquaintances but not many friendships. So we want to explore the levels of friendship and take a look at how to achieve genuine friendship. There is an old sick joke that relates to this: one man says to the other, "No, you are not my best friend. Maybe my best acquaintance, but not my best friend."

Sometimes people have different perceptions of the friendship relationship. For example, some people are very unaware of themselves, their surroundings and their effect on people. Their antennae are not refined enough to see that people are bored when they talk; people have heard their stories; and people are tired of their shallow conversations. Some of these folks make an assumption that they are best of friends with people who are reflective and interested in growing, whereas the latter do not have the same perception of the relationship.

Another factor is that the needs of two people might be entirely different. One might need people to whom he can talk, whom he can trust; the other might only need a golfing partner. This kind of relationship simply is not going to have intimacy. Or, one might have deep emotional and spiritual needs because he has not acknowledged some hurt in his past…and that need has certain anti-social effects in his relationships because the other person has already dealt with such issues in his own life. There will be a lack of intimacy between these two individuals.

And of course, there is the whole macho barrier to close male friendships. Men are often taught they are born to be unfeeling, aggressive, risk-taking etc. But in fact, ideas and practices related to masculinity and men's nature have changed a great deal over time. Books by Kimmel (**Manhood in America**, 2005) and Rotundo (**American Manhood**, 1993) have capably demonstrated how malleable masculinity really is. Men are influenced to develop in certain ways much more than simply being born this or that way. In fact, during the past several decades, space has been cleared for emotional expression among men through social movements such as *Mythopoetic Men, Promise Keepers, Million Man March* and what many call the *New Fatherhood*, which stresses caring, doting and involved dads. Thus, there is room for men to make important changes in their lives and friendships.

We say a lot more later on, but it seems to us that we use the term friend much too loosely and in an almost cavalier manner. We have heard speakers say to audiences of hundreds of people, "Friends, I want to say you today…" and then begin the speech. How can all those people be friends? The fact is—they cannot be. So the word friend is cheapened and downgraded.

Solomon makes a distinction in Proverbs:

Proverbs 16:28 A perverse person stirs up conflict, and a gossip separates close friends.

Proverbs 22:11 One who loves a pure heart and who speaks with grace will have the king for a friend.

Epiphany

John has had a meaningful career as a minister, seminary president and author. Jim told him he thought the over-arching conceptual strength to most of his messages centered on conforming to the image of Christ. Christ set the perfect example and was therefore the perfect role model—though impossible to follow to perfection.

As John continued to ponder and study this subject of friendship, he considered the earthly life of Jesus. Jesus lived as a man and had friends in His human experience. Why not learn from the Perfect Friend how to be a friend—both in word and action? Why not, as the Apostle John instructed, "Walk as Jesus did while on earth" when it comes to friendships.

When John shared that idea with him, Jim had an epiphany: Why not study Christ's friendship behavior (e.g., with the disciples) and reverse engineer it into principles for friendship? We recognize Jesus as the God/man—fully God and fully human. However, we do not think of Him as one of the guys because He was The Guy, The Man of all men, i.e., the Lord, the Son of Man, the Savior. And yet His followers observed Him in a diversity of normal and human situations and learned from Him. Thus, we can learn from observing Him in every incident and every interaction with others during His earthly life. We see in Him and in His relationships with His men the standard and substance of what a friend can and should be.

That is the approach used to write this book. In Jim's work as a business professor, he focuses on helping organizations achieve high performance through transformational leadership, team building and technology. We arrived at the title of this book through the idea that learning from Christ relating to His friends could be the basis for **Achieving High Performance Friendship**.

Consider the relationship of the apostles to Christ. After He was crucified, they went into hiding. They were scared men. But after the resurrection, they become bold and determined. One of the most compelling reasons for our faith in Christ is that all of these same men suffered a martyr's death for teaching the Good News—except for John, who died in exile (**Holman Bible Dictionary**, 1991).

What changed them from fearful men in hiding to bold men proclaiming Christ's message? Simply stated, they had the confidence-inspiring experience of seeing the resurrected Christ—compelling and overwhelming evidence that their Friend was indeed the Son of God. This took friendship to a holy level. Why else would they risk death teaching the message of Christ as He had instructed them? They were all changed men. Many say Peter's change was the most dramatic. He was transformed from a man whose primary goal to save himself led him to deny even knowing Christ three times before Christ's crucifixion. Peter had ample warning: after being jailed by the Sanhedrin (Jewish religious leaders) and seized by Roman King Herod, he escaped before he was crucified in Rome sometime in 60 AD. Even so, these warnings did not detract him from boldly telling the story of why Jesus Christ came to earth.

We chose high performance to characterize high-quality friendship. In this context, performance connotes the unusual, responsive, extraordinary and superlative. Performance is a term most men relate to well. For Jim, high performance fits his friend Howard McCreary well. Howard is a real *motor head* who loves and owns high performance cars, and his friendship is a personification of one. Howard keeps an eye on Jim's properties in New Mexico, and whenever Jim calls on Howard for a favor, Howard is so responsive Jim has to be careful not to abuse the friendship—like a car that has excessive horsepower. A modest request results in more than an ample response.

To further illustrate, when we step on the gas while trying to pass an 18-wheeler on a two-lane highway, we don't want an anemic, sluggish response—we want high performance. Similarly, none of us want an anemic, sluggish response from a friend when we are in need of physical, emotional, psychological or spiritual support.

What do we mean by high performance friendship? Perhaps the best answer is to provide the litmus tests we apply to our own friendship. To us, a friendship is high performance if both friends:

- take the opportunity to provide selfless acts on behalf of the other
- feel comfortable sharing inner-most thoughts, yet respect the other's private thoughts
- trust the other with that which they hold dear
- support each other when one falls short or fails, and readily grant forgiveness
- appreciate and accept heartfelt constructive criticism
- truly celebrate each other's success without jealousy or envy
- sustain the relationship in spite of distance or time
- refrain from making or tolerating any disparaging remarks about the other, especially behind his back

As for disparaging remarks, consider this:

Few friendships would survive if each one knew what his friend says of him behind his back.

> ~ *Blaise Pascal*

If it is very painful for you to criticize your friends–you are safe doing it. But if you take the slightest pleasure in it, that's the time to hold your tongue.

> ~ *Alice Duer Miller*

Both of us treasure that we have always shared our concerns about the other in each other's presence. Sometimes this was done with caution, but it was always with the best of intent. We are embarrassed that we can't claim that for all friendships throughout our lives, but it is a principle we endeavor to live by today. We believe that if we can't say it to your face, we shouldn't say it behind your back.

Earlier during this project, a number of men's study groups asked permission to use our working draft of the book as part of their ongoing group work. We gratefully obliged. One group leader communicated that after reading the introduction, many in his group felt discouraged. They commented, "We certainly don't measure up as high performance friends." Some disparagingly acknowledged they were pathetic at friendship. The comments were similar to the story told by John Feinstein is his book **Moment of Glory: The Year Underdogs Ruled Golf** (2010). Mike Weir, as a rookie said, "I thought I was making pretty good progress with my ball striking until I watched Nick Price. I realized I was so far away from where I needed to be it was almost a joke. I stood there and said to myself, 'Okay, what you've been doing isn't good enough.' I have to find a way to get better."

Have you ever noticed we rarely achieve more than we set out to achieve? The purpose of this book is to inspire us all to raise the bar on the quality of friendship we share—to high performance. Nevertheless, since we are using Christ as a standard, we must accept we will never match perfection. However, if we strive to conform to His example of friendship, can we not help but greatly improve?

Christ-like Principles for Friendship

Our methodology to derive friendship principles from Christ is to draw from His statements and behavior in the Gospels. In addition, we believe Christ is the embodiment of all wisdom. The Bible's book of Proverbs is a book of wisdom, providing a foretaste of Christ before His birth. As such, we draw from it as another source to derive friendship principles.

Our hypotheses proved true. We found powerful and compelling principles for high performance friendship. Since the book is about using Christ-like principles for friendship, we use CHRISTLIKE as an acrostic for convenience and simplicity as follows:

C   **Choice of Friends**
H   **Humility and Honesty**
R   **Respect**
I   **Intimacy**
S   **Support**
T   **Trust and Teach**
L   **Love and Loyalty**
I   **Independence and Internal Compass**
K   **Kindness**
E   **Encouragement and Eternal Values**

Each of the principle categories from the acrostic represents a chapter in this book. In each, there is a definition of the principle, stories to illustrate it, lessons from Christ's approach to friendship and prescriptive thoughts on how to apply Christ-like behavior to your friendships. This structure enables you to read and reference chapters in your order of preference.

For readability and convenience, Bible references are not cited within the text of each chapter. Rather, they are included at the end of the book under Index of Bible References, organized by page number with a topic indicator. So if a page contains a Bible reference, paraphrase or quote, the reader can find the reference under that page number in the index.

The constructs within the CHRISTLIKE acrostic are highly interdependent and synergistic—the sum is far greater than the parts. For example, is it not easier to Love someone whom you Respect; who is Kind to you and Supports and Encourages you; who you Trust to share Intimate feelings and thoughts? But rather than discuss all these constructs at once, we develop each one in a separate chapter and then bring them together in a Summary at the end.

Some years ago, John was listening to music and realized that the musicians had moved from one song to another without any break or change of pace. He listened to the song over and over trying to discern how they did it. It was as though one song went away as the next song began slowly. It was as though a two-color sweater (blue on top and gray on bottom) did not have a break in colors but a slow blend of the weaving from one color to the other.

John sent Jim the song and asked him how the musicians did it. Jim, a musician, understood. He explained that the musicians stay in the same key and rhythm while making a subtle transition to a different song that uses the same chord structure...they subtly soften the first song, and as it fades they gradually bring in the new one until it is in full swing.

This exemplifies how we see these ten qualities of Christ blending in harmony. It is not as though we might have seven of the ten and therefore think we are doing better than someone who has only four. Rather, we blend all of the Christ-like qualities. One may be needed and then it fades out as we need another to step to the forefront. Then that quality can relax and fade to others that come to the forefront as situations require. This is why we say they are interdependent and synergistic.

Quite honestly, until we began this project, we did not see this interdependence and synergism. But as we discussed it, we came to realize it is true. Friendship is more than liking someone; it is loving him, wanting the best for him and helping him grow—just as Christ did with His friends when He walked the earth. We found that our friendship deepened; we learned and grew a great deal personally from studying and writing this book. We wish the same for you as you seek to develop your own high performance friendships.

In the spiritual life, nowhere do our ideals meet the actual more truly than in how we relate to each other, in how we make, sustain and are friends.

~ James Ishmael Ford

What Makes This Book Different?

There are a multitude of books targeted at men in Christian book-stores. These are usually sole-authored books written by profes-sional ministers that include whole sections on men's spirituality. We wrote this book to be quite accessible whether the reader is a person of faith or not. Though we point to Christ as a role model of friendship, we are doing so from His human experience. Those who question Christ's deity rarely question His skill as a great moral teacher and a source of much learning.

We are two people who deeply care for one another, challenge one another, help one another grow and love one another. We occupy very different professional and social worlds and our experiences differ considerably.   Nonetheless, we hope to provide a unique complement of perspectives that prove to be useful. Our book is truly dialogical. As such, it emerges from the similarities (and quite notably) the differences between the two of us that we hope you find both interesting and instructive. In this sense, the book pro-vides a model for how men can connect with one another both on points of commonality and points of difference. The approach is pragmatic—not where "the rubber meets the air" (*remember, the authors are a professor and a pastor*), but where the "rubber meets the road!"

Collaborating on this book taught us much about friendship and each other. We ended up far deeper friends than when we set out because despite seeing weaknesses, we also uncovered strengths in each other that we had not seen before we began writing togeth-er. We hope this book is as meaningful to you and the friends with whom you share it.

Chapter 1

Choose Friends Wisely

A true friend is the most precious of all possessions and the one we take the least thought about acquiring.
~ Francois de La Rochefoucauld

What is a friend? Friendships sometimes happen almost by chance. We meet someone, we like them, and over time a friendship is established. But more often than not, we make a decision to choose someone as a friend. When that friendship is established, we recognize the relationship as our being attached to another by affection or esteem. Or, as more poetically expressed by Aristotle, "A single soul dwelling in two bodies."

Men need friends in their lives. Friends provide love, support and companionship. Friends are a crucial connection to our human experience that fulfills many of our needs. When we achieve high-performance friendships, they are an important frame of reference we use to calibrate and learn about our behavior, allowing us to grow.

Friends can reinforce each other with positive or negative direction, but we recognize that peer pressure happens, not only among our children and our friends, but also among adult men. It can be subtle and negative. Or it can be direct, loving and positive. We recognize that among men peer pressure is part of that calibration and should be a powerful and uplifting force. We have seen, since both of us serve or have served on boards of directors, how friendships develop in the corporate setting and how peer pressure can be enormous.

Enron is one of the most hideous corporate financial scandals in recent history. Peer pressure was a culprit. A colleague, Jeffrey

Pfeffer, of Stanford University, spoke of Robert Jaedicke, a former Stanford accounting professor and chairman of the audit committee of Enron, and stated:

Those who know Jaedicke well pose this question: how could this ethical, honest, and decent man have been caught up in such a massive financial fraud? There are many possible and plausible answers, including the fact that responsibility can become diffused when many people are present and observing an action (e.g., Latane and Darley, 1968), in that no single individual may feel particularly responsible or comfortable with disagreeing with the others.

Peer pressure isn't limited to boards of our major corporations; it is part of our daily activities and relationships. Thus, we men must know who we are; we must know what our values and standards are; and we must know who those men are who would try to shape our thinking and modify our behavior into what they want us to do and think. If we do not know who we are, we capitulate and become someone we do not want to be and should not be. Though peer pressure is real, it does not have to define who we are.

We are well served by positive friendships and, as we mature, we learn to discern those that are not positive. Sometimes that results in painfully having to choose to end a friendship that is not positive, while taking care to cherish those friendships that inspire us to be better. And we contend that those friends who would try to shape us by subtle peer pressure should be left behind. At the same time, we are not best served by choosing only friends who think like we do. Friends who think alike can fall into what can be a dysfunctional dynamic called group think. We humans are lousy intuitive statisticians, which is why many of us throw money away buying lottery tickets or gambling in places like Las Vegas. We generalize way too easily. For example, when we have a bad experience on an airline and conclude that it has bad customer service all the time, we swear to never fly that airline again.

If we surround ourselves only with people who think the same way we do, we are statistically misled into thinking our point of view (unchallenged) is more valid than it is. That's how a lynch mob can do something the individuals in it would not otherwise do. It's also how a religious group can develop a sense of superiority and become judgmental. Because of this phenomenon, C.S. Lewis insightfully observed, "the worst part of Christianity is Christians."

Having friends who believe and think differently than we do is instructive and helpful so that our conclusions are better challenged and, therefore, likely to be more substantive. We have learned through experience the error of not listening and considering those challenges. In his book **Faith Logic: Getting Online with God** (2007), where he makes a logical argument for God's existence, Jim asked his atheist friends to review and critique his work, to ensure it was properly challenged. As a result, the book was stronger by responding to those challenges.

We do, of course, need friends who share our beliefs and values so they can challenge our moral compass should it stray off course. Research into individuals (e.g., Bernie Madoff) who stray horribly off course and make destructive decisions has shown that they do not have a trusting friend to challenge them and thereby hold them accountable. We (John and Jim) treasure our friendship because we are comfortable in challenging each other on even trivial issues without fear of the other realizing that nothing more than loving concern is being expressed. Political, business and religious leaders can achieve so much power that no one dares challenge them, which can lead to their eventual demise (e.g., Saddam Hussein, Jim Bakker—PTL). Power corrupts; absolute power corrupts absolutely.

We refer to Saddam Hussein and Bernie Madoff because they are well recognized villains. But we all experience acquaintances in our immediate sphere of influence who, left unchallenged and not held accountable, stray off course. A little power can intoxicate an otherwise positive person into one who becomes unpleasantly dictatorial. In John's world of ministry, there is a saying that is probably more true than any of us want to imagine: "Once a man becomes a bishop, he never again will eat a bad meal or hear the truth." In Jim's world of academia, professors have been known to use their field of expertise as a way to avoid listening to others by saying, "I am the expert in this field." This is why we need friends who care enough to confront us and tell us the truth.

Have you ever had a friend or boss who said, "Please feel free to provide candid feedback if you don't like what I am doing," only to be punished when you tried? At one of John's annual reviews, he was asked what his aspirations were for the future. He answered that he wanted to be a regional director. His boss affirmed this aspiration. When the boss was dismissed, John was promoted. Later, a man who reported to John came to him to ask his forgiveness. With tears in his eyes he explained that after John was promoted he had been party to gossiping about John. He explained that John's former boss came to visit him and said that John always had coveted his position...and he did not stop the conversation. John had answered a straightforward question about his aspirations in the review, but apparently the affirmation of those aspirations was not as sincerely received as John thought. The man who reported to John was sincere in asking for forgiveness, which John gave. When John asked his former boss about the conversation, he denied it had happened.

The lesson to be deduced from this anecdote is that a good litmus test of a friendship is the ability to provide caring, well-intentioned feedback and the ability to receive caring, well-intentioned feedback.

As the Introduction explains, each chapter focuses on a friendship theme pertaining to achieving high performance friendship and has several stories that reflect on it. Here are a few of our own experiences.

The Pastor and the Professor – Jim

It is fitting that the first story be one about how the two of us became friends—a friendship that has lasted over 30 years, even though we have lived in different cities for over 20 of those years.

I had recently moved to Minneapolis to accept a position on the faculty of the University of Minnesota. Church attendance had not been a priority the first couple of years in Minnesota, as we had a two-year-old and a newborn, but we felt it was important to get active again. My parents had moved to Minnesota with us from Houston, as they needed family support due to their own failing health. They also wanted to be near their grandchildren, so we found them a home close to ours—we could all have our space but still be near each other.

My parents were attending a suburban church in west Minneapolis where John was pastor. My mother kept encouraging me to come listen to John, which, ironically, worked against my attending. My mother was a woman of beautiful faith and Bible knowledge but we just weren't on the same page when it came to faith. I can be strong-willed and spiritually challenged in faith matters. My mother believed so easily, not hampered by the logic required by my computer programming professorial mind. To illustrate, she fell and broke her leg one night getting up to get a drink of water. Her view of the story was that the Lord was watching over her because she fell by the phone, making it possible for her to call 911. From my logical perspective—which I never shared with her—if the Lord was looking out for her, why didn't He allow her to avoid the object she tripped over in the first place?

The point? If she liked a particular pastor, he would most likely be more to her liking than mine.

Nonetheless, I reluctantly attended a service and was immediately drawn to John as someone from whom I could learn. He spoke calmly, assertively and logically as he delivered his message. His presence and style of delivery were similar to many executives I had consulted with over the years. I have told John, and still maintain, that he could have been a very successful business man. John's tongue in cheek response was that he couldn't afford the cut in pay.

John's message that day was straightforward and can best be described as how we should and can conform to the image of Christ. In subsequent messages, the topic was different but the theme of conforming to the image of Christ was consistent.

Although as a child I spoke of being a minister—exciting my mother to euphoria—when in college and having my faith challenged, I struggled to determine what was truth or fiction in matters of faith. Had I been a minister, I would have loved to come across with the sincerity and credibility of John.

When I first met John, I had just finished a complete study course of the Bible, as I strived to achieve spiritual resolution. I felt by developing a friendship with John, I might have some profound conversations. So I set out to become friends, and John was responsive.

There was a crowning development in our friendship when I made a proposition to him. As part of my faith quest, I wanted to go to Jerusalem, which I consider corporate headquarters for the big three religions of the world—Judaism, Islam and Christianity. But I wanted trusted instruction as part of the trip. So I offered John an all-expense-paid trip to the Holy Land if he would be my tutor and promise to answer any question I asked in his trademark, straightforward manner. He agreed and we went. It was an extraordinary experience that took our friendship to the next level.

Some compelling things he shared with me include that he had also gone through an agnostic stage, just as I had. Then he clarified that he was an ordinary agnostic—one who doesn't know if God exists but would like to find Him—as opposed to an ornery agnostic, who doesn't know if God exists and doesn't want anyone else to find Him either.

When I asked John why God doesn't just communicate to us directly, John responded, "He does, if you pay close enough attention." (I found that to be true, but more about that later.)

The Pastor and the Professor – John's Response

I like to tell the story—which is not true but is good for a laugh—that the first time Jim approached me after a service, he said, "If all the people who slept in your sermons were laid end-to-end, they would be more comfortable." Actually, from my point of view, I was meeting so many new people in those days, people who were trying out our church, that I tended to limit my time to people whom I thought would get involved. I focused on people who would help us grow the church or who had asked for help from one of the other leaders or me to meet a specific need in their lives.

One of the professors where I attended seminary had an axiom, "Do not become friends with people in your church." I did not agree with that statement when I heard it, and I do not agree 40 years later. But the fact is a pastor cannot be friends with everyone. In many cases, he cannot even know everyone. But as a strategic thinking pastor, he can make sure everyone is covered and having needs met through networks of small groups.

I did, however, know Jim's parents and thought highly of them. So when they introduced me to their son, I was delighted to meet him. Jim is pretty humble about his accomplishments, so I had to drag out of him what he did besides teach as a professor at the University of Minnesota. It turned out he was a prolific author and ranked as one of the top dozen information consultants in the country.

As Jim and I began to talk, however, I realized this was a relationship that would be good for me in a number of ways, so I relaxed my self-imposed restriction and made time for us to chat. I liked him and we clicked. He had expertise from which I could learn, and he was willing to learn from me. It soon became apparent that he was interested in me for personal reasons that went beyond the pastor/parishioner role, and thus began a great friendship.

One day, he came up after my sermon and said, "Your sermon was very helpful to me. Thanks." Then he smiled a devilish smile and said, "I am going to give my speech to three different audiences in three different cities this week for a pretty good honorarium. You have to create something brand new for this same crowd next Sunday. How do you do it?"

I knew then that he understood the rigors of studying and creating a brand new sermon every week for the same audience. His affirmation and compliment meant the world to me.

Close Shave on Our Friendship – John and Jim

In retrospect, there was a bizarre situation that could have derailed the possibility of our friendship before it ever developed—if we hadn't quickly developed trust in each other.

Jim was giving a breakfast speech at the Sheraton Hotel located between the Twin Cities of Minneapolis and St. Paul. The absent-minded professor rushed out of his home to navigate the morning rush hour traffic. As Jim was being introduced to guests attending his presentation, he reached up and stroked his chin. To his chagrin, he realized in his hurrying he had forgotten to shave (that is the absent-minded part).

Embarrassed but creative, Jim rushed to the gift shop and purchased a disposable razor and shaving lather. He then sped to the bathroom, untied his tie and shoved paper towels around his collar to protect his clothing from the water of the forthcoming shave. Jim had just lathered up and was about to take the first stroke of his face when he heard a familiar, but puzzled sounding voice, "Jim, is that you? Why are you shaving in here?"

Jim, like a deer in headlights, realized he was facing an interesting communication challenge when he saw John's reflection in the mirror as he stood behind him.

How do you explain to your pastor, who is in the same hotel for a pastor's conference, why you are shaving in a hotel bathroom a few miles from home?

As Jim tried to explain, the two of them started laughing so hard they could hardly breathe. We have laughed again many times in the retelling of the story over the years. The debate remains about who laughed the hardest. But an emerging friendship went to the next level that momentous morning.

Real Friends Don't Use Peer Pressure – John

One of my first experiences of choosing friends carefully was watching some of my buddies in high school. Some of them had started drinking…and they targeted one particular athlete to get him to drink.

I was never a target. Alcohol had no appeal to me, probably because I had watched alcohol ravage the lives and careers of three uncles.

Later in college, some fraternity brothers were encouraging me to drink alcohol. We were having a bull session one night and the pressure intensified just a little. Finally, I said, "Okay, give me one good reason to drink and I will." The room got real quiet and then one of the guys, who later became an attorney, said, "You can dance better." I laughed and said that if that were the best reason they could give, I would not drink.

My decision never offended them or changed our friendship. Alcohol simply does not appeal to me. Their drinking does not bother me. And as far as I know, my abstinence does not bother them. However, if I did have a problem with alcohol, I might be forced to choose between my friends and sobriety.

Back in high school, one of the guys kept at another. His trump card was to say, "You are too chicken to drink with us." That was the magic word. Chicken got him. He said, "I am not chicken," and started drinking. He succumbed to peer pressure. Sadly, about fifteen years later he had become an alcoholic, and it ruined his career. As I have gotten older, I have come to realize that peer pressure is often more subtle among adult men than it is in high school or college. But it is real. If a person is immature, he often cannot tolerate any differences of opinion, and communicates that he wants people to agree with him. Conversely, I have watched people not tell the truth in board meetings because of peer pressure; they simply cannot stand against it. Jim provides more remarks about boards and peer pressure in Chapter 8.

Rock or Not – Jim

When I was a junior in high school, my mother went to Colorado to earn a Master's Degree in Special Education. Rock and roll music had become a major social phenomenon from the influence of such groups as the Beatles and the Rolling Stones—and I was interested in participating.

I had taken piano lessons for a few months in grade school, and my older brother, Bond, had taught me how to play by ear. I transferred those skills to learn how to play the guitar, bass and piano. To my surprise, an established group heard about me, asked me to audition and offered to provide me with an electric keyboard if I would join their band. It was too good to be true—until my mother forbade it. She was worried about the lifestyle dynamics of being a rock musician. I was frustrated beyond belief.

After mother graduated, we returned to New Mexico, and my parents reluctantly allowed me to start a band with friends I had grown up with that my parents knew and trusted. I started teaching each one of them how to play an instrument—I played lead guitar and wrote a few songs. We had an exceptional senior year playing for dances and concerts. We even cut a record that got some regional radio play. (In a book that includes references to Christ, I must candidly admit we weren't that talented—but we were loud!)

My rock band buddies were great friends and still are. However, none of them were as committed to school as I was. We talked about all of us attending the same college to keep the band intact. My inner voice told me that if I did, my chances of succeeding at college would be too compromised by the distraction and temptations that would be part of having a rock band.

It was a difficult choice—my friends and the band or my education? I painfully dropped out of the band and deliberately went elsewhere to college. My friends had a great time but dropped out of college the first year. Though they have had fulfilling occupations and lives without completing college, I made the right choice for me, and they allowed me to make it—that's what good friends do.

Temptations are Personal – John

One of the difficult challenges in choosing friends is evaluating whether a friendship might have an adverse affect on us. There is no one right answer. The issue is whether our friends are helping us grow or leading us in an unhealthy direction. For example, if drugs, gambling or sexual immorality are a temptation, choosing friends who also are inclined to fail in our areas of weakness is not apt to be in our best interest—unless the friends are members of a support group organized to overcome a problem (e.g., Alcoholics Anonymous). Temptations are different for all of us, which is important to understand when choosing friends or potential friends. Friends can bring out either the worst or the best in us.

My father was a fine Christian man. He was an elder in his church but he also had some friends who were absolute reprobates—they drank and they womanized. He went on golfing trips with them; he loved them, but they did not have an adverse effect him. Indeed, at Dad's funeral, one of the reprobates came to my mother and said, "If I ever decide to become a follower of Christ, it will be because of what I have observed in your husband's life."

In retrospect, I realize my father was being a friend to his troubled buddies by his example. Since he did not share their temptations, he could spend time with them in a manner that would be unwise for some. Rather than judging friends who succumbed to temptations that were not an issue for my father, he kindly tried to show a better way.

Wrong Priorities – Jim

The summer I was 15, we moved into a new neighborhood within the same town. I wasn't able to drive legally, so proximity was a key factor in choosing friends. Next door was a nice kid a year younger than I and a grade behind. Charlie and I spent most of the summer together as we shared interests, primarily in boats, and even dreamed of having a boat marina someday.

Charlie was a good kid—honest, open and loyal. But I had a problem. As summer drew to an end, I realized we would be returning to school and Charlie would naturally assume we would continue our friendship at school. I already had friends at school that were my age and in the same freshman class, though a couple of them were older, as they had been held back a year. I became concerned I might be socially penalized by the in crowd as a result of my younger friend Charlie hanging out with me.

Even more troubling to me was that I was concerned that Charlie would not be cool enough in the eyes of my older friends. Charlie did, in fact, need a serious wardrobe update, as his clothes and shoes seemed influenced by the cartoon character Charlie Brown. What did I do? Something stupid and selfish is what I did. Just before school was to start in the fall I fabricated a disagreement with Charlie to use to end the friendship. How pathetic!

I will never forget Charlie, showing so much more integrity than I did, looking me directly in the eye and saying, "We're not friends anymore because of that?" Whatever it was—I don't even remember—it was that shallow.

After Charlie's sincere question, I knew I was so wrong and had to make it right. I apologized and decided the solution was to help Charlie become more cool. I asked him about the boyish shoes he wore, and he confided that he hated them. They were his old Boy Scout shoes, and his mom would not buy new shoes until the old ones wore out. Accordingly, we proceeded to wear them out. His mother discovered us in the backyard as Charlie was kicking the crap out of boulders to damage the shoes. It was slow progress; those well-made Boy Scout shoes had a double leather toe-shield. But once Charlie's mom understood the problem, she was amused, and new shoes were forthcoming. She was a great mom who realized her little boy was going through some changes.

In short, Charlie turned the corner on cool, such as it was. Later, he became the bass player in our rock band, and because he was a year behind the rest of the members in the band, he went to college a year later and did just fine.

He is still a lifetime, loyal friend and an accountant who does my tax returns—that's trust!

The other friends I feared losing if Charlie hung out with us are mere acquaintances today. I am so grateful that I got my priorities right and am able to count Charlie a best friend decades later.

Funny thing—I called Charlie and asked permission to use this story in the book after again apologizing for my behavior. He didn't even remember the ugly part of the incident. He did remember those ugly shoes and kicking boulders until his feet hurt.

Driven Away by Arrogance and Cynicism – John

I was fourteen years old and in the eighth grade. I had been elected Student Body President of my grade school. One night, I was asked to participate on a panel at a PTA meeting. I do not remember what I said or who else was on the panel—except for Virgil Langtry. Mr. Langtry was actually Judge Langtry, a State Circuit Court Judge for the county. After the meeting there was a social time and Judge Langtry spent most of the time sitting in the cafeteria talking to me across the long rectangular tables we used then. He was not in a hurry; he was completely focused on me; he talked to me about leadership. I was fourteen years old but he made me feel as though I was the most important person in his life. I specifically remember my parents waiting patiently in the hallway without any sense of signaling me that we needed to hurry up and leave. I believe they were proud of the attention Judge Langtry gave to me that night.

Later, when I told my mother's brother (who would become a Public Utilities Commissioner for the state of Oregon) about the experience, he scoffed at Judge Langtry giving me that kind of time and attention. He dismissed the judge, the judge's abilities and reputation (they were outstanding because later he served on the Oregon Court of Appeals) and the time he gave to me that night as being "political." I am not sure how the time could have been political because fourteen year old boys could not vote then and still cannot vote in Oregon.

I learned plenty that night and in subsequent conversations with that uncle about friendship. I realized he always had to be right; he did not care if he was disrespectful to his wife, my mother or my father. It seemed as though no one could do things as well as he could. Even city hall and highway crews never got it quite right in his estimation.

I learned by observing my uncle that friendships don't develop when overbearing arrogance and cynicism are present. Those leave little opportunity to share one of the great dynamics of friendship—learning from each other. And as I have reflected on his life, I do not remember that he had any friends. I wonder if that was because life and all discussions had to revolve around him.

Over the years, I have observed that it does not matter if a person is educated or uneducated, sophisticated or unsophisticated, Christian or non-Christian. The best friendships develop when both parties are humble enough to realize they have something to learn from each other and that deep friendships do not develop the way they should unless we listen to others.

Achieving high performance friends means choosing well.

Christ's Approach to Choosing Friends

Not all temptations are as obvious as something like adultery. Both of us have had men talk to us about the small print of endeavoring to be Christ-like. They have talked to us about the arrogance and negativity they sense in some of their would-be close friends—Christian and non-Christian. It is all very subtle...always being right regardless of the subject, not listening to another point of view, making sure the conversation always revolves around them, not being teachable and often criticizing others—especially those in political leadership. These attitudes are antithetical to how Christ lived and acted when He was on earth. The Apostle John said Jesus was "full of grace and truth." The grace of God is a gift from Him that is freely given, though undeserved. As Jesus extended grace, He was serving to make people better by helping them grow and improve. Grace serves the purpose of helping people grow in whatever area of life they need to grow. So whether we are talking about the grace of God directly or God touching us through someone, we become better by being touched by Him. And not only was Jesus full of grace, He was also full of truth—no smoke and mirrors, no half-truths. Grace and truth are a package—one does not seem to work without the other.

One man said it this way: "I realized certain friends were dominating in their arrogance and cynicism. They seemed to take joy in their sense of superiority. I felt guilty by association. They would not listen when I tried to raise the issue, so it was best to end the relationships." As a respected colleague observed, "There are people who act as if they are the foremost authority on everything."

In Jesus' parable of the sower, there is useful insight that we can apply to friendships. Farmers in Jesus' day were not educated and did not use today's sophisticated farming techniques. When a farmer wanted to plant a field, he walked through the field throwing (sowing) seed so it covered as much of the tilled ground as possible.

In His parable, Jesus used this practice to explain that the seed does not always fall on fertile soil. Sometimes the seed falls on dry ground and dies. Sometimes, it takes hold, begins to grow and then dies. It is true in relationships and friendships as well. Some relationships never grow into friendships. But just as the farmer has to sow the seed, so men have to extend themselves to make friends.

One of the greatest and most compelling models for friendship is expressed by Jesus when He says, "Do unto others as you would have them do unto you." Interestingly, as a pastor, John has spoken on these verses often. For effect, at times he has stopped the presentation and asked the audience to convey how they like to be treated...and how they do not like to be treated. As they respond, the answers are projected on a giant PowerPoint screen. Some of the things people have said relative to how they want to be treated are: respectfully, fairly, equally, graciously, lovingly, kindly, patiently, caringly, honestly and gently. They have also said they want to be accepted, appreciated, validated, trusted, valued, understood, heard and encouraged.

Jim does a similar exercise when he is conducting executive education on leadership. He asks the audience what they expect from their leaders. He then asks the audience what their leaders should be able to expect from them.

What is easier to consider: how do I like to be treated or how I should treat others? Which list do you think is easier and more quickly developed? We are egocentric beings that tend to put ourselves first, which is a barrier to developing deep friendships.

The way we want to be treated is how we should treat our friends. Pure and simple. The Apostle Paul expands on this when he writes about Christ giving up His position in heaven. He says, "Christ did not consider equality with God a thing to be grasped but laying aside His deity took on the form of humanity." We believe Jesus was divine when He was on earth—He was the God/man—but He was willing to step away from heaven and come to earth to show us how to live.

From this great historical truth of Christ's heart and love for mankind, the Apostle helps us see Jesus as the model for friendship. He instructs us to "not be selfishly ambitious or conceited; be humble and see other people as better than ourselves. We should look not only to our own interests but also to the interests of others."

Because each of us has needs in the area of spiritual growth, it is fair to ask if a relationship or friendship makes us a better person. Solomon gives great wisdom on this subject when he writes, "My son, if sinful men entice you, do not give in to them." Solomon also writes, "If you walk with wise men you will grow and if you walk with fools you will suffer".

Men like to make fun of each other, put one another down and often do not let even the slightest miscue pass, but Jesus' model moves us in a different direction. The writer to the Hebrew Christians expands our understanding of Jesus' words that we should treat others as we want to be treated when he writes these words: "We need to be thinking and considering how to stimulate our friends to do loving acts and good deeds for others."

This is a tough question, but one that we all need to ask ourselves: do we consider how to stimulate our friends to be better people?

The word, *consider*, connotes giving deep thought to the matter, as opposed to a cursory thought. Maybe an even tougher question, then, is to ask whether we think our friends are considering how to stimulate us to be better people?

Principles for Choosing Friends

Just as the sower has to throw the seed on the field, so we need to initiate and extend ourselves in making friendships. And we have to keep our value system in place, asking ourselves if this is a relationship that is going to help us grow spiritually.

Solomon is clear when he writes, "Do not make friends with a man who loses his temper easily or you might learn his bad habits and get in trouble; if sinners entice you, do not succumb to them...a perverse man stirs up dissention and a gossip turns friends against friends." Although Solomon is writing specifically to the issues of anger, entrapment and gossip, there is a larger principle as it relates to friendship. We must ask ourselves if our ultimate goal in life is to become conformed to the image of Christ—to become Christ-like. If it is, then we have to evaluate our friendships and ask ourselves whether our friends are having a positive or an adverse affect on us. There is no one right answer. The issue is whether our friends are helping us grow or hindering our spiritual growth.

Francis Schaeffer said the spirit of the age always finds its way into the church. By this, he meant there are certain attitudes and behaviors in society that we seem to adopt, almost by osmosis, because they are so prevalent. They are not right and they are not Christ-like, but they are so common we simply fail to see them and often begin to use them. They can be gossip, pride, arrogance, cynicism, negativity, irritation, anger and lack of forgiveness.

Thus, as some have said, we have to "have the newspaper in one hand and the Bible in the other." We are aware of society and we are aware of what Christ-likeness is. And when there is a conflict that is injurious to our being Christ-like, we have to choose Christ-likeness.

Theologians have wondered for a long time if Jesus made a mistake when He picked Judas to be on His team. We think it is safe to say that no one knows. Nevertheless, there is a vital principle that we learn from Jesus' handling of the relationship once He learned Judas was going to betray Him. In modern English, He cut His losses. We often placate people or hope something will develop in a relationship when it won't. When Jesus knew Judas was going to betray Him, He was quick to the point and said, "Judas, do what you are going to do." As it relates to the parable of the sower, we do not know which relationships will take root and which ones will not. We meet someone and we like him. We think there might be a mutual benefit in the relationship. We initiate a second step and find that we enjoy him. But at the third step, we discover there is no real compatibility. And we have to move on. That is just the reality of trying to make friends. Or we initiate the second step and he never returns the call. We try again...with the same result. We cannot spend all our time worrying about it. We move on.

When we realize a friendship is not going to develop and be mutually beneficial, it is best to quit calling or pretending it is a friendship. This does not suggest there is anything wrong with either person. Sometimes there simply is no *simpatico* between the two good people. John learned this when he was asked to be on a seminary board. A good friend of his, "Bob," had another good friend, "Jack," who was also on the board. John was looking forward to meeting Jack. Unfortunately, after becoming acquainted, it soon became obvious that John and Jack were not simpatico. John said to Bob sometime later, "Jack and I have not clicked." Bob answered, "Yes, I understand. Jack told me the same thing." There was no criticism and no gossip—just the reality that in relationships not all levels are the same. But it was handled honorably.

Friendships grow out of similar likes, compatibility and needs. Friends meet needs in the lives of their friends. Friends help their friends grow. We are responsible for seeing and discerning what will be helpful or harmful to us. Thus, it seems that we must have the freedom to unchoose certain people as friends if the relationship is injurious to our becoming more Christ-like. This might be obvious for socially unacceptable sins such as drugs, alcohol abuse and adultery, but not for more common and socially acceptable sins such as negativity, gossip, criticism behind one's back, arrogance, a know-it-all attitude and nit-picking. If our friends refuse to deal with such sins in their own lives and they are dragging us down, we might need to unchoose them.

If our highest ambition is to become Christ-like, we must have friends who help us on that quest. Jesus says, "if a person has ears let him hear" in reference to people understanding and wanting to be involved in the kingdom of God. Although He is talking about the kingdom of God, we can draw an important life principle from what He says. It seems that some men do not have ears for spiritual growth and becoming conformed to the image of Christ. The compelling question is, "Do I want to grow in Christ?" If the answer is yes, we need to make sure there are friends in our lives who are helping us grow. We need ears to hear and our friends need ears to hear. It is more than church life and activity. It is having ears to hear.

There is no better way to show a friend that we care about having a high performance friendship than by listening. And there is no better way to show we are sincere about friendship than to listen to his answers when we ask a friend for his advice. As someone said, "It is hard to start an argument when you are listening and not talking."

The Apostle James tells us that we should be, "quick to listen and slow to speak" as a way of showing our love for others. Genuine and loving friends take the time to listen to their friends; listening is more important than speaking in high performance friendships.

Our friends are an important choice. To develop high performance friendships, we need to take the time to give considered thought about who we befriend and with whom we choose to remain friends.

Discussion Questions and Applications

1. As we evaluate our friendships, do our friends make us better people and more like Christ, or do we just enjoy being with them?

2. Do you know men who seem always to draw attention to themselves or have to be right? Do you know men who often seem to be negative? Does this stem from insecurity? How is it unlike Christ? What kind of an effect do they have on us?

3. As painful as it would be, are there some friendships we need to leave or unchoose?

4. Who are the friends who consider how to stimulate us to love and do good deeds?

5. How do we evaluate ourselves relative to considering how we stimulate our friends to love and do good deeds?

6. Can you recall a time when you sowed a seed that reaped a friendship?

7. Is there someone with whom you could sow a seed and see if it reaps a friendship?

8. What stories about good and bad choices in choosing friends can you share in a helpful manner with your friends?

9. Would your friends say you are quick to listen and slow to speak in your relationships with them?

Chapter 2

Humility and Honesty

Humility is the solid foundation of all the virtues.
~ *Confucius*

Honesty is the first chapter in the book of wisdom.
~ *Thomas Jefferson*

High performance friendships are based on good communication. Humility and honesty are two constructs that naturally link together and facilitate good communication in friendships. If we honestly assess ourselves, how can we help but be humbled? We all have strengths and weaknesses. Our strengths come from natural talent and hard work, through education and experience.

Jesus modeled genuine humility when He washed the feet of His disciples the last time He met with them in the Upper Room in Jerusalem before He was crucified. Because streets were dusty, a good host always had a pitcher of water and a cloth for his/her guests to use to wash their feet. Jesus went beyond the norm; He knelt and washed His friends' feet—even the feet of Judas who was about to betray Him. There is no greater expression of humility toward one's friend and we can learn from His example.

A good friendship allows us—if we are honest and humble with each other—to offset our weaknesses by drawing from each others' strengths. For example, as co-authors, we accepted Jim's strength in creating architectural format and organization of the book as he had previously written thirty books. Conversely, we accepted John's strength in Biblical matters as a pastor. We deferred accordingly. Nonetheless, even with our respective expertise, we needed to be humble enough to accept an honest suggestion from each other whether expert or not. Sometimes, less expertise creates awareness of a flaw in the thinking of an expert, especially a human one.

As we shared the draft with friends, we also needed to be gratefully humble and honestly accept feedback and suggestions from diverse perspectives and expertise—even though it meant more work for both of us!

We have both worked in academia, where we often confuse focus with genius. When you are in a classroom teaching the same material to students who have yet to learn it, you can delude yourself into thinking you're brilliant. Yet it can be quite amusing to watch a professor of nuclear physics get outsmarted and taken advantage of by a car salesperson. The professor buys a car only every few years. The car salesperson sells several cars a week. Who has the focus advantage now? Thus, focusing on the strengths and abilities we have in one area might well preclude us from asking if the constructs of humility and honesty are indeed a part of our complete selves.

We humans can be such unbelievable idiots at times. Where we get the notion to be prideful should be a mystery to us all. Jim's daughter, Jamie, inadvertently conveyed an important lesson about humility: When she was only five years old, one of her friends inquired, "Your Daddy is a doctor?" Jamie calmly replied, "Yes, but not the kind who can do you any good." Ouch!

A humorous saying is that "arrogance is God's gift to the superficial." No wonder we find so many atheists among college professors! We often hear professors say they can't accept Christianity because it isn't intellectual. It is implied that only the uneducated or those with low IQ's believe in Christianity. Yet like a parent who loves all his or her children regardless of how talented or bright, the beautiful thing is that a loving God does the same with us. As different children connect with parents in different ways and at different levels, so it is with God.

Of course, arrogance is in conflict with humility and honesty. Can we be arrogant and humble at the same time? Or be truly honest? Are you more impressed by someone who brags about his accomplishments or someone who is humble? Sometimes, in our efforts to impress by bragging, we accomplish just the opposite. Have you noticed how impressed we tend to be with those who first convey the feeling that they are impressed by us?

Have you ever accidentally knocked over merchandise in a store? There are two responses to this situation. First, a person accelerates his pace to remove himself from the scene of his crime—a hit and run—as if nothing happened. The second is the one who, though embarrassed, stops and picks up the mess he created. Which of the two do you think impresses more people, the first or the second? You guessed it. Research shows people are more impressed with those who demonstrate humility and honesty and take responsibility, even if it is embarrassing.

Mac Davis, a recording artist who had a twisted sense of humor, wrote and recorded a spoof song entitled, *Lord, It's Hard to be Humble*. The key verse was:

> *Lord, it's hard to be humble,*
> *When you're perfect in every way*

Let's see what we can learn from a few of our stories about humility and honesty.

Humility: An Alternative to a Bloody Nose – Jim

One of the realities of growing up male is that sometimes you have to come to blows in order to defend yourself or your pride, ego or manhood. Being tough has certain social advantages and some, including bullies, enjoy exchanging blows to make a point, or perhaps, more to get attention. Unfortunately, some men never learn that tough is not a favorable behavioral attribute as they attempt to use bragging and intimidation as a dynamic among their male friends.

I never found getting in a fight to have much of an upside—especially after a bigger guy bloodied my nose when I was eleven.

When I was thirteen, I moved to a new town and had to take the bus to school. There was one kid who hung out with his gang of buddies who soon realized I was the new kid and took great pleasure in taunting me. In my immaturity, I would have taken him on, but I was certain if I got the better of him, his gang would jump in, so I had a no-win situation.

I grew weary of the daily humiliation, and one day, as a new kid, I asked the gym coach for some advice. This would never be acceptable in today's politically correct world, but what he proposed, I appreciated at the time. He said, "You tell Robert he can meet you in the gym after school. You two can put on some boxing gloves and get the matter settled."

What a relief—a fair fight with adult supervision! I went to Robert and told him of the opportunity to solve whatever issue he had with me. He looked at me and waved me away and said, "Just forget about it." He never bothered me again.

But my friend Jimmy Evans had a better way. We were best friends from the time we were five until he abruptly died of a blood clot when he was 18. The loss had a profound effect on me. Perhaps it is one of the reasons I treasure friends as I do.

Jimmy was an extraordinary athlete, but more significantly, he was as open and outspoken a Christian as I had ever known. Quite frankly, I was more of a closet Christian—active at church on Sunday but keeping a low profile otherwise. Had to be cool, you know.

Jimmy lost his father to heart disease when we were seven, and I think that triggered a stronger commitment to faith in him. The thing that was so different about Jimmy was that in spite of his athletic success (e.g., leading basketball scorer in the conference), he was unbelievably humble. He actually had scriptures on humility from Proverbs posted on his bedroom wall.

To my knowledge, Jimmy never had a physical altercation with anybody. How did he avoid it? Humility and honesty!

When some tough guy would challenge Jimmy with the typical rhetoric such as, "Hey, Evans, I could/should/will kick your butt," Jimmy, who was not a puny guy, would humbly say, "Good grief, I wouldn't want to fight you. Look at the guns on you. No doubt, I would incur some serious damage. What can I do to keep peace with you so we can avoid that?" Now, Jimmy could have handled himself well in a fight, but he was smart enough to know that no one leaves a fight unscathed and fighting was not consistent with "turning the other cheek."

It worked every time. We knew the outcome of any fight would likely favor Jimmy but his humility and honesty kept him out of the fray. The bully would be flattered and Jimmy could diffuse the situation, often creating a friend.

Am I not destroying my enemies when I make friends of them?
~ Abraham Lincoln

Jimmy had an amazing talent for "turning the other cheek" without ever taking a blow. It greatly reinforced that he was committed to a Christ-like life.

When he died at eighteen, the funeral service could not accommodate all the teenagers who attended. Many had to stand outside. Jimmy was an amazing example of humility who touched so many lives.

Humility and Honesty from a Trusted Source – John

My brother, uncle, his friend and I were golfing. We were joined at the turn by our mother and sister. We needed to make room on one cart for our mom so she could ride with our uncle, and room on another cart so our sister could ride with my brother. No one was making anything happen, so I stepped into the gap and took control…very kindly and gently, I thought.

Suddenly, my older brother was behind me and whispered into my ear, "Who made you the general?" That was his very gentle way of saying, "Back off, baby brother. We can get this resolved without you turning it into a military operation."

Yet when our mother died, we were all at the viewing the night before her funeral. The funeral home was getting ready to close, and my brother wisely realized that we family members needed a few minutes alone. Some guests and well-meaning people were not taking the hints that we wanted the final few moments before closing to be just for family members, so he asked me to solve the issue—knowing that I could get it done—which I did.

However, it was not easy because I had to go to people who loved our mother and were grieving her death, and tell them that we family members needed a few minutes alone with Mom's body before the mortuary closed. This is one of the reasons I love and respect my brother so much and value him as one of my best friends. He understands my strengths but he does not excuse the excesses of those strengths.

In these two incidents, I saw both the humility and the honesty of my brother. He is humble enough to figure out how to correct me and tell me to back off without making a scene or embarrassing me. Indeed, no one knew he was talking to me. Yet he was honest with me and avoided the natural temptation to complain and gossip about me to others.

After the golfing incident, I said to him, "Hey, Mike, that was really good how you handled that." He looked at me, smiled and said quietly, "Yes, and you needed it."

At the mortuary, on the other hand, he was humble and honest enough to realize he does not like confrontation, so it was easier to ask baby brother to be the one to ask people to leave. Then he could lead us in prayer while we were alone with Mom's body for the last time.

We belabor this point because we believe knowing ourselves and growing into Christ-likeness are two of the key elements of being a good friend. We also believe that each of us has blind spots and we need friends who are willing to love us enough to tell us about them. However, if our primary goal in life is to be active, to be achievers in the marketplace or public square instead of becoming Christ-like, we can never achieve the humility and honesty that are needed.

We all need other people to tell us things that are obvious about us but which we do not see. Some are blind spots where we need improvement; some are positives. I remember one time a friend was talking to me about my penchant for being too abrupt. He asked, "Do you ever listen to yourself?" I had not thought about that, but his challenge was the impetus for me to start doing so.

Servant Leadership – Jim

Coach Al McGuire led his Marquette basketball team to a Cinderella national championship by upsetting North Carolina in 1977. He had an insightful perspective on leading young men. On an airplane flight we shared, he told me that the most difficult part of coaching was watching nineteen year old boys run up and down the court with your paycheck in their mouth!

It was a statement on the limits of power of a head coach.

There are two basic schools of thought on power—top down and bottom up. Experienced leaders learn that people can reject leadership power by not affirming a leader through lack of cooperation and passive aggressive tactics (Bernard, 1938 and 1968). Great leaders become servant leaders by learning that serving first is the secret to leadership success (Greanleaf, 71, 91,02).

Fortunately for my older brother Bond, he learned the lesson quickly when he was nineteen and in Air Force boot camp. He was given leadership of the troops in his barracks, which included ensuring his barracks could pass the scrutiny of inspection. Nothing like being responsible for something others don't want to do and you can't do by yourself. How do you get the rest of the troops to cooperate? Humility and Honesty. When the rest of the troops went out for recreation, Bond stayed behind, working late into the night to clean the barracks spotless—even scrubbed around the toilet bases with a toothbrush. The next morning when the troops looked around, they were surprised and impressed. Bond said, "This place is ready to pass inspection. We can keep it that way if we all cooperate. I can't do it without your help. Can I count on you?" It worked.

I was only fourteen at the time, but my big brother had given me one of my first lessons in leadership. The next year when I got a job managing a Laundromat, I was paid 75 cents an hour and was told that if I did a good job I would get a raise to 85 cents an hour (yes, I am that old). The washing machines were in need of a major cleaning, so drawing from the lesson I had learned from Bond, over the next few days I cleaned, polished and waxed all the machines just as I had done on the car I was paying for with my job. My boss walked in two weeks later and was so impressed he gave me the raise to 85 cents immediately.

Many years later, when I was on the board of Best Buy, I watched Brad Anderson take over as CEO from Dick Schulze, the founder and iconic legend of Best Buy. Brad had worked in the very first store with Dick and had been his side-kick for the amazing journey of becoming the number-one consumer electronics store in the world (**The Best Buy Story**, 2011). I didn't envy Brad. Dick was an extremely difficult act to follow and many members of the board had reservations.

As a young man, Brad had set out to become a Lutheran minister and retained the values of a man of faith, which served him well in his new role.

As in most businesses, what is working today has to be replaced by something new and better tomorrow. Accordingly, the first thing Brad did was to study and learn everything he could from books and industry leaders so he could ensure the proper direction for Best Buy's future. He came up with a new strategy aimed at better knowing and serving their customers, called customer centricity. Though he had included his management team in the exercise, there were those who showed support to Brad's face but were passive aggressive behind his back. They were going through the motions but were not accepting Brad's leadership.

Through Best Buy, Brad had achieved financial success beyond his wildest dreams—especially since his initial plan was to be a Lutheran minister. But money was never a primary motivator for Brad. Like Dick, he found meaning through adding value and making a difference in people's lives.

Brilliantly, Brad started awarding his stock options to team members who were best helping Best Buy achieve the new strategy. This generosity set a compelling example of Brad's leadership and was so refreshing compared to the greed for which many CEO's are known. Other managers wanted to follow Brad's leadership example and be able to allocate at least some of their options to their staff.

Did it work? Oh, yeah. Brad's new strategy was successfully implemented.

One of Brad's team members who didn't buy in left Best Buy to become the CEO of Circuit City, Best Buy's major competitor at the time. He was not a servant leader in my humble opinion. Within a few years, Circuit City was gone.

In 2004, Brad's warm smiling face graced the cover of *Fortune Magazine* when under his leadership Best Buy was named the Company of the Year. Not bad for a humble, honest leader who, by the way, would have made a great minister.

More Common Than You Might Know – John

At age fifteen, I was walking home from Babe Ruth Baseball All-Star practice when a neighbor man stopped and asked me if I wanted a ride home. What fifteen year old kid would turn down a ride? When we got to my house, he suggested we go get a milk-shake. What fifteen year old kid would turn down a milkshake?

After getting the milkshake, we headed home, but he stopped his car along a fairly isolated area and told me he wanted to show me something. He pulled some pornographic pictures out of his wallet and showed them to me. Then he propositioned me—in very graphic terms.

To say I was scared would be an understatement. Not knowing how he would respond, I told him, "I think you better take me home." I watched him very closely because I heard what a good street fighter he was; he had gone to high school with my uncle (the golfer), who had told me all about it. If he reached for me, I was going to jump out of the car and run through fields to get home. I knew he could not have caught me. But if I had jumped out of the car, I would have left behind my shoes, glove and bat. So it was a perplexing and frightening situation.

Thankfully, he put the car in gear and took me home. Not another word was spoken. And in spite of the fact that our houses were less than a mile apart, I think I saw him only one more time in my life.

I continued in athletics in high school; I was a student body officer; I did not lack for affirmation. After college, God gave Susan to me, and we married when we were both twenty-three. Yet, there was a lingering doubt as to whether I was sending off some signals of being effeminate because of the man's proposition. Interestingly, I never told anyone about that experience until I was twenty-nine.

When I became a pastor, after ten years in campus ministry, I began telling about that experience to help others who might have been hiding such an experience. The first time I told about the experience in Minnesota, Jim came up after the sermon and said, "That man sexually abused you." I said, "No, he did not. He never touched me." Jim diplomatically held his ground and firmly restated that I had been sexually abused. From Jim's statement and later conversations with sexual abuse counselors, I learned that intimidation, whether verbal or physical with sexual intentions, is sexually abusive.

Jim's coming up to me was a great expression of friendship. He could have backed off when I said very firmly that the man had not abused me. But Jim did not back off. He held his ground. That is what good friends do—they take risks to help their friends. I could have rejected Jim's comments but he offered them anyway.

More Common Than You Might Know Includes Me – Jim

We often don't realize that what seems to us a minor conversation can be significant to a friend. Two experiences from my youth had motivated my comment to John after his sermon.

When I was fourteen, there was an eighteen year old senior, "Bob," who attended our church. We had evening youth services, and afterwards, Bob would drive boys and girls around in his car (we weren't old enough to drive), which provided us an opportunity to socialize. In particular, two couples could squeeze in the back seat, one couple in the front, and make out while our *chauffer* drove us around. He would drop off each of us at our homes—girls first, boys last. On one occasion, I was the last to be dropped off. Bob took me for a longer ride saying he wanted to show me something.

We ended up in the middle of nowhere, and then he stopped the car and encouraged me to participate in sexual activity with him. Suddenly, the fact that he never had a girl with him and his willingness to run us around for no apparent reason became clear. I was not sure how Bob would handle rejection. Would he verbally assault me for being ungrateful for his generosity? Would he physically assault me? Or would he just kick me out of his car in the middle of nowhere in treacherous terrain to walk home in the dark? This was prior to cell phones, so a walk home would have taken three or four hours and my parents would be frantic. Fortunately, he accepted a diplomatic rejection and he gave me a ride home. I never got in his car again.

The second experience happened when I was sixteen and a junior in high school in Colorado. My mother was going to graduate school and I went along. As a new kid, I had all the challenges of making new friends. "Gary," another junior, extended friendship to me early on and we started hanging out together. Within a couple of weeks, when we were hanging out in his bedroom, he suggested we engage in a physical relationship. I never saw it coming but quickly rejected the proposal. He tried to persuade me with the argument, "How can you knock it if you haven't tried it?" It was an arrogantly made argument. I told him I had no desire to even try it. Fortunately, he backed off, but our friendship ended.

Both Bob and Gary were dishonest in the guise of friendship. Friendship does not involve ulterior motives. The difference was that Bob's engagement was abusive. He had placed me in a circumstance where I felt I was potentially in physical danger if I did not cooperate. Gary, though dishonest, pressured me in circumstances where I could and did leave. I felt betrayed that under false pretenses he took advantage of my being a new kid who wanted to make friends. Bob's behavior is considered abusive because of the threatening circumstances. I never felt in harm's way in the Gary experience, so it was not abusive. It was an insightful distinction that helped me understand the difference I discerned in the two experiences, which is what I shared with John after his sermon.

We have both chosen to share these stories because you may have been affected by someone trying to take advantage of you when you were a kid. As we stated in the headings for our stories, it is more common than you may know. Our advice is that you should keep the secret no longer. Talk to a close friend. Perhaps some of the thoughts shared in Chapters 4, 5 and 6 on Intimacy, Support and Trust, respectively, can be helpful. Our stories are told to demonstrate how some who act in the guise of friendship are not true friends. But as John and I benefitted from sharing our experiences, so can others.

Even a Pastor Can Offend an Attorney – John

Susan and I have a very close female friend who was going through a divorce in California. It should have been a simple deal, but her husband was determined to squeeze and negotiate in order to make her as uncomfortable as possible. One time, he even sent a bill for nine dollars for the kids' health insurance. He hired one of Hollywood's most expensive divorce attorneys. My advice to her was to "hire the best Jewish attorney that you can find."

Later, when I was interviewing for the pastorate of Bethany Church, I told that story in an open question and answer forum. When the meeting was over, a man waited for me, and after introducing himself, said, "I am a Jewish Christian and I am an attorney. Your story was offensive to me." I explained what I meant, i.e., that I think Jewish attorneys are family oriented and would be offended at the husband's behavior and therefore fight vigorously on behalf of our friend.

He said he understood my motivation and heart but explained that my words, however sincere, were offensive and easily misunderstood. Then he shook my hand. I thought, "I am going to like this man because he is honest." Today, I am honored to call David Harowitz one of my best friends. He is a gift to me. Our friendship started because he did not gossip; he did not distort; he told me the truth. And he told me the truth in a way that made me understand that his motivation was not to put me down but to make me a better person. And I was interviewing to be his pastor!

Compare David Harowitz's edifying and affirming challenge to me to remarks from others who have seemed less interested to help with a correction or wished just to be hurtfully critical. Once, I had a friend sneer at me that I had a character defect. This was about who he thought I was rather than concern about behavior improvement. In cases such as this, the motivation does not seem to come from goodwill and a desire to facilitate growth but rather to put me in my place.

And, whereas David was full of grace and truth, some of his opposites have been full of vile and opinions. Whereas David's behavior drew me to him, their behavior has pushed me away. David demonstrated humility and honesty; the others did not—with predictable consequences for friendship possibilities.

Pride Does Come Before the Fall - Jim

Earlier, I mentioned my rock band. To be clear, I was better at the business side of music than the music side, which is probably why I am a business professor and consultant today. But I did have a life-altering lesson in humility from the days in the band.

Having your record play on the radio when you are on a date can give you serious delusions of grandeur, as does getting well-paid for playing in front of a few hundred kids at a university dance, as we did the night before we played for free at a charitable event the following day.

We were foolishly impressed by the revenue and success of the night before and actually regretted that weeks earlier we had agreed to a freebie. We showed up and behaved like arrogant little punks who were giving a much larger gift than we actually were. Worst of all, we lowered our effort level to match the lack of payment. Our performance was well below par.

The Beatles song *Money* was popular, and we performed it half-heartedly and laughed while we sang the lyrics: "The best things in life are free, but you can give 'em to the birds and bees, give me money… that's what I want…give me money." We thought we were clever; singing the song in what we thought was a humorous manner, since we were not getting paid.

After that performance, we noticed a sharp decline in our bookings. We didn't know why until we learned from an honest older friend that word had gotten around about how disrespectful we had been at the charitable event. We had to rebuild our reputation very carefully and slowly after that mistake, which we never made again. Ironically, we gave several benefit performances as part of our redemption efforts.

I carried the lesson forward when I became an author and international speaker. By the way, a speaker has the same business model as a musician: books are your albums, and a speech is a gig, where you use your PowerPoint presentation instead of a guitar. On occasion, I am asked to speak gratuitously, in lieu of an obscene honorarium. The humility lesson was learned from the rock band days—it is not honest to agree to a gratuitous speech and give anything less than if you are being paid your top fee. It is dishonest to agree to an event if you are not going to give it your best.

High performance friends are humble and honest and help keep us humble and honest as well.

Christ's Approach to Humility and Honesty

Jesus' washing of the disciples' feet as they entered the Upper Room shows great humility on His part. He took on the form of a servant; He put on a loin cloth; He bowed to wash their dusty and dirty feet when they should have reversed the picture and bowed to wash His feet. As the God/man, Jesus was able to be honest and humble. He knew Who He was. He did not have to perform or posture for adulation.

Jesus and His humility are inspiring when we think about His washing the feet of the disciples, calling out His disciples for ignoring a child, and in particular, His dying for our sins. Furthermore, Jesus' autobiographical sketch is huge as it relates to friendship. He knew Who He was; He knew what He was about. He explained His relationship to the Father and His commitment to following His purpose on earth when He said, "My sustenance is to do the will of the Father."

Near the end of His life, He prayed, "Father, I have accomplished all You have given me to do." Although we will never reach the state of perfection of Jesus, it is our contention that self-understanding is necessary to be a good friend. But self-understanding has to be the recognition of who we are because of how God made us—not who we are on our own merits.

Jesus speaks to this issue when He talks about talents. We believe He is saying we are all born with a certain number of talents. Some are one-talent people, some are five-talent people and some are ten-talent people. The Apostle Paul explains this when he writes that after Jesus departed, He sent people with gifts of being apostles, evangelists, prophets, pastors and teachers to the church. Paul also says that the people Christ continues to send need to utilize their gifts to the fullest for the body of Christ to grow.

The Apostle writes, "What are you so puffed up about? What do you have that God hasn't given you? And, if all you have is from God, why act as though you are so great, and as though you have accomplished something on your own." We must recognize that everything we have is a gift from God. It is our responsibility to maximize the talents God has given us, while giving Him the credit for them, and yet be humble because we realize He could have given those gifts to someone else. This kind of an admission engenders humility and honesty because we realize we are no better than our gifts and that we are no better than anyone else.

Not only does Jesus say He is humble but He also says He is gentle. Gentle should not be confused with weakness. Gentle was a word used in three different contexts in Jesus' day:

1. A soothing medicine on an upset stomach
2. A cool breeze on a hot day
3. A strong, powerful horse under the control of his master (power under control)

The word gentle is also used by the Apostle Paul when he explains it as one part of the Fruit of the Spirit. In other words, the quality of gentleness that describes Jesus is not a human-developed quality but a Christ-like quality. Jesus said it was to our benefit that He return to the Father, for when He did return, He would send the Spirit. One of the roles of the Spirit is to build Christ-likeness within us; and one goal of His work is to build the gentleness of Jesus into us.

From Jesus' words, we learn more about Him, and we see principles for our friendships:

1. He knows who He is
2. He is not trying to impress anyone
3. He is our friend and shows us how to be friends
4. He has something to contribute to us
5. He does not expect perfection from us

We see such honesty in Jesus as He walked the earth. He wept. He grew tired. He got angry when He cleansed the temple in Jerusalem of money-changers who had violated it as a place of worship, and He struggled with the pain He was going to suffer when He would be crucified.

Jesus talked about "taking the log out of your eye before you take the speck out of your friend's eye." This is genuine humility—not worrying about another person until we have taken a deep and penetrating look at ourselves. Taking an honest look at our own imperfections and sin, then realizing that God still loves us cannot help but make us humble.

The Apostle Paul helps us understand that the humility that Christ wants to build in our lives has an outward effect—it affects how we treat and respond to others. We are not only to be humble but also gentle, patient and forgiving. This is being Christ-like.

Principles for Humility and Honesty in Friendship

When we acknowledge that everything we have is a gift from God—when we are honest about it—we begin to be humble. The easiest way to admit this is to acknowledge that none of us achieves the standard of Jesus in our lives.

Often, when men get together, there is little humility. Rather, there is a great deal of posturing and bragging—not unlike gorillas standing in the jungle beating their chests to let others know who is the strongest. Seldom do you hear men drawing out one another and really listening to other men. The need to put down the other guy— even in fun—is a little like the male lion eating newborn males to stamp out the competition. One man told us that some of his friendships are very little about sharing and helping one another— they are all about competition and one-upmanship.

But Jesus was not this way. He never played the gorilla in the jungle to draw attention to Himself. And He does not want us to be this way either. We cannot take credit for what we accomplish, because we are only manifesting the gifts God gave us. Having this attitude lends itself to having the kind of humility that God wants us to have.

Thus, the man who seems to have the need to talk about himself OR put down others OR rarely draws out others, simply underlines his seeming lack of humility and his need to bring attention to himself. Men look for affirmation from the wrong place at the wrong time.

Solomon says that we are to "let the lips of another praise you." So when we brag about ourselves, not only are we violating the words of wisdom from Solomon, we are also likely covering up some insecurity in our lives. And have you noticed, it is more convincing when others praise you?

Which is usually the more honest assessment: the one we make of ourselves or the one made of us by our friends? Have you ever noticed that people who can be honest about their own strengths and weaknesses are generally more effective people? If our self-assessment correlates to that of others, we are more realistic about what is possible in our relationships. For example, are we better served if we acknowledge we have a quick temper than if we deny it?

Jesus was able to make an honest appraisal of Himself, which allowed Him to be honest with God the Father, with Himself, with His followers and with us. As hard as we might try to honestly appraise ourselves, we fail because we are not perfect. This is where the help of friends is invaluable—if there is honesty among us. When friends are honest with each other, constructive feedback can facilitate more accurate self-appraisals. We can then be more honest with God and ourselves about our shortcomings and our needs, leading to greater spiritual growth.

John had an experience that illustrates in a humorous manner our need for feedback from friends. He was on an international flight to China and brought prescribed sleeping pills to help him sleep. As the flight departed, he took a couple of pills, which usually put him to sleep quickly without any unpredictable responses, although others have had them. Later, thinking the pills were not working, he took another one.

When he woke up, the pills were missing from his briefcase. He asked the woman next to him if she knew if someone had handled his briefcase. She curtly responded, "Ask the flight attendant." The flight attendant told him she had taken the pills and would not return them until after they landed. Stunned, John realized he must have behaved in a bizarre manner. Too embarrassed to ask what happened, he quietly returned to his seat.

Without feedback, he had no way to know what he did while under the influence of sleeping pills. It remains a mystery to this day. He sure wished there had been a friend with him on that flight! And he wished he had been courageous enough to ask the attendant what he had done. The principles are clear: we need friends to tell us, and we need to ask our friends to tell us honestly where we need to grow.

John says that in forty-six years of ministry, he has met only two people who claimed to be perfect; one was crazy and the other one was lying. Isn't it ironic that we can readily accept that we are not perfect like Jesus but we can be a lot less humble at the same time? Jim teaches in a Physicians MBA Program. One of their favorite jokes is this: if you ask a physician to name the top three people in his field, he will have a difficult time coming up with the other two names.

Our self perception is so easily distorted. If we are not careful, we may base much of our identity on our careers and monetary achievements. Just as drugs or alcohol allow the abuser or addict to avoid dealing with reality, so the person who fails to take a deep and penetrating look at himself can use his worldly activity to avoid the reality of his need to grow and become more Christ-like.

A drug counselor we know says that frenetic activity allows people to stay in a state of denial and to avoid looking at themselves relative to where they need to grow, just as getting high enables the abuser or addict to avoid introspection and how he needs to grow and improve. If we are busy working, we can convince ourselves by concluding, "I cannot be that bad because of all the good work I am doing, all the people I am helping and all the money I am giving."

Jesus did not bring obvious attention to Himself—He was comfortable with Himself. Jesus was the embodiment of Solomon's words to "let the lips of another praise you." Jesus never praised Himself. When He was asked if He claimed to be the Son of God, He answered quietly and without fanfare, "It is as you say."

When friends have the need to bring attention to themselves, they do themselves a disservice. Thus, we need to consider how we can stimulate them to love and do good works without self-promotion. We need to care for them.

We both feel blessed to have friends—including each other—who challenge us by their honest appraisals. It does not feel wonderful at times, but it is useful. We both find the more humble the source of the honesty, the more readily we accept it.

Humility breeds honesty and honesty breeds humility.

Humility is not thinking less of yourself; it's thinking of yourself less.
~ Rick Warren

Discussion Questions and Applications

1. Why would humility be a foundation for all virtues?

2. How are humility and honesty interlinked?

3. What are the obstacles to honesty in a friendship?

4. Do you find it easier to be critically honest about a friend to a third person than to your friend directly? What is the risk to friendship?

5. Even though John and the Jewish attorney became friends, how would you coach John to express his intentions with less risk of offense?

6. Jim mentions his rock band and the pride the guys felt when they did a concert pro bono and did not perform to their standards that night. If you were a good friend of Jim's in the audience, what would you say to him during a break to help him?

7. Humility comes from recognizing that all we have is a gift from God. Why, then, do you think so many men seem to need to bring attention to themselves for what they have accomplished and what they do?

8. Jesus knew who He was and could say to the Father at the end of His life, "I have accomplished all You gave me to do." How does that challenge us as men to invest the gifts and talents God has given us?

9. What stories about honesty and humility can you share in a helpful manner with your friends?

10. Although we do not walk dusty roads today and do not need to give our guests a pitcher of water and cloth to wash their feet before they enter our homes, are there ways we could humble ourselves to "wash the feet" of our friends?

Chapter 3

Respect

Consult your friend on all things, especially on those which respect yourself. His counsel may then be useful where your own self-love might impair your judgment.

~ Seneca

Respect pertains to esteem or sense of worth or excellence of a person and his behavior. For example, we might respect the manner in which a friend handles a difficult situation. Showing respect to someone we love and appreciate is not usually a challenge. An obstacle, however, might be the temptation to covet the admiration a friend is receiving. In a moment of weakness, friends might feel resentment and somehow try to diminish the respectful admiration of a friend by calling attention to a flaw. Alternatively, friends can become competitive and attempt to redirect the admiration in their direction by giving reasons that their own accomplishments are as worthy as those of the respected friend.

But healthy high performance friends truly celebrate when esteem is bestowed on their friends.

Usually the larger challenge is respectfully coaching a friend's behavior that is not in his best interest. It takes courage, diplomacy and respect not to shy away from this responsibility in a friendship. Ironically, correcting a friend in the proper way is a useful way to earn respect because you are doing him a favor worthy of respect.

This is well illustrated by the following quote:

It is one of the severest tests of friendship to tell your friend his faults. So to love a man that you cannot bear to see a stain upon him, and to speak painful truth through loving words, that is friend-ship.

~ Henry Ward Beecher

Have you ever heard the saying, "Keep your friends close and your enemies closer?" What does that mean? Does it say that our enemies speak about us more clearly and honestly than our friends? Does it warn us that our enemies are apt to reveal our weaknesses more readily than those who might be motivated to please us—to a fault? Would we be better served by receiving constructive criticism provided from honest friends?

Don't believe your friends when they ask you to be honest with them. All they really want is to be maintained in the good opinion they have of themselves.

~ Albert Camus

If you had a choice, would you rather that people respect you or like you? Can you really like someone you don't respect? Achieving balance between like and respect can be challenging. Are there times we sell out our principles to participate in a questionable conversation to fit in and be liked?

And of course, is it not a destructive form of disrespect to lack the courage to share a concern with a friend but instead share (gossip?) about it with others?

A response of judgmental superiority does not earn respect. Sometimes we can be guilty of spiking the ball when someone transgresses—almost relishing the opportunity to correct another person. Purity of motivation, authenticity and diplomacy are key in earning respect when correcting a friend.

An early marker of a good friend is that he not only respectfully acknowledges our good works but also helpfully and truthfully encourages us in areas in which we could and should do better.

Truth springs from argument amongst friends.

~ David Hume

True friendship can afford true knowledge. It does not depend on darkness and ignorance.

~ *Henry David Thoreau*

Let's examine a few stories and then see what we can learn from Christ about respect.

A Professor with Business Protocol – John

In the early stages of the development of our friendship, there was a defining moment of mutual respect that seemed trivial at the time, but it advanced our friendship to a higher level.

I got a call from Jim at church one day, and after checking to see if I was busy, Jim asked, "John, are you aware of the double layer of secretaries it takes to reach you?" I wasn't sure what he meant, so I asked him to explain. Jim continued, "When I call your office, the first secretary answers announcing the church name. When I ask to speak to you, I am told that I will be connected. But instead, I am put through to a second secretary announcing I have reached John Vawter's office and asking who is calling. John, since you come across as unpretentious and accessible, do you think this seems more like the protocol executives use to screen out unwanted interruptions?"

I was unaware what callers were experiencing and I certainly didn't want anyone who called to feel like I was church CEO instead of the church pastor. More significantly, I was impressed that Jim not only took the time to call the matter to my attention but also respected me enough not to leave me in the dark about a procedure that could distance me from the very people I wanted to be close to—members of the church congregation.

I made it a point to thank Jim and compliment him for the manner in which he handled the matter. Jim acknowledged he was concerned that I might take offense and that perhaps I would think that he should mind his own business. He said he felt there was some risk, but if I was as genuine as he perceived, it was worth it. That little conversation paid huge dividends in our emerging friendship. Have you ever tried to help a friend with constructive suggestions, only to experience the proverbial "Kill the messenger?" Over the years, Jim became an extremely useful resource. As a professor and renowned speaker, he offered helpful words of encouragement and suggestions after sermons.

Most recently, my receptivity to the conversation about my church bureaucracy paid off as we co-author for the first time. This is my third book, but the first with a co-author. So I told Jim we had taken a vote for general manager on the project and the vote was 30-2. When he asked what I was talking about, I said, "You have authored thirty books. I have done two. You need to be in charge."

Jim laughed and explained to me that his years as a computer programmer helped him with his writing discipline. After working with me, he made an observation about my writing that was most helpful. He said, "John, you have a gift for speaking with a compelling stream of consciousness. Your ability to reference scripture is humbling to me. That stream of consciousness which helps you as a speaker creates a bit of a challenge in your writing as I integrate your text into the book. Are you open to some feedback that will help the book move along?"

Based upon past experience with Jim, I knew his motivations were pure and my authoring would benefit from his suggestions. It did—I hope you notice. For example, he explained that readers are less forgiving if the progression of thought isn't clear, whereas a listening audience always has a chance to ask questions. He pointed out that our social contract with the readers, as established in the introduction, is to have stories and then draw upon Christ's lessons. I had been inserting Christ perspective into the stories whenever moved to do so, as I would in a sermon—stream of consciousness.

As I thanked Jim for respecting me enough to provide feedback, he explained, "John, you have written two fine books on your own.

Ordinarily, I would be reluctant to be so candid with a new co-author. It is only because you have respected my motivation in the past that I was comfortable to encourage you to do even better."

Used to be My Town – Jim

James Taylor wrote a painful song about the end of his marriage with Carly Simon entitled *Used to be Her Town*, which expresses well the heartbreak experienced when a marriage ends in divorce. The lyrics include: ...*"Someone said something 'bout, something else someone might have said...Well, people got used to seeing them both together but now he's gone and life goes on.... Some of them his friends, some of them her friends, some of them understand, Lord knows that this is just a small town city, yes, and everyone can see you fall, It's got nothing to do with pity..."*

I have been through a divorce that was heartbreaking for my family and friends. It's unfortunate that over 50% of marriages end in divorce. Many good people get hurt. During this crucial time, friendships are tested and many don't survive.

My former wife and I have both remarried and have happy marriages that resolve the issues we could not resolve as a couple. And I take responsibility for the failing.

But the point of sharing this painful story is to talk about how shared mutual friends responded. Some friends and family took sides, and others, like John, were able to show love and respect for both sides. John had a particularly interesting challenge having been a pastor and friend to both my former wife and me. Had he taken my side, he might have lost my former wife as a friend and lost a certain amount of respect from me. Why? Because had he done that, he would have been disrespectful to someone I still care about and disrespectful to me to suggest that was something I wanted.

Alternatively, had I actually expected him as a man friend to take my side, I would have lost his respect and not have deserved his friendship.

John was respectful to me and my former wife by being supportive and loving to both of us. He told both of us that he would protect all confidentiality and never be a conduit for either of us, and he has kept his word.

John was Christ-like in that he was never judgmental and was always transparent and honest in his actions. For example, when he was a guest pastor in a church that was within geographic distance, he invited both my former wife and I to visit but made sure we were both aware of the invitation. And after John and I agreed to write this book together, out of respect for my former wife, he made sure she was fully informed and made sure I was informed he had done so.

No surprises, but plenty of respect. He never expressed his friendship better than during that difficult time.

May We Talk About Me? – John

Jim and I both enjoy listening to conversations between men wherever we go. It seems to us that many conversations are not dialogue, but a monologue where one person seems to bring every aspect of the conversation back to himself. When my son, Michael, was five years old, I took him out for our weekly date. We were in his favorite ice cream restaurant, and across the room a man was talking about his business conquests so loudly that the entire room could hear him. In typical little kid fashion, Michael quieted things down when he looked at me and said, "Daddy, why is that man talking so loud?" I thought (and still think) I knew the answer—he had a need to impress us all.

I remember listening to a conversation on an airplane in the row behind me. It was not as though I was eavesdropping; rather it was as though the man wanted everyone to hear. (He is probably a cousin to the man in the ice cream shop.) I counted the conversation going fifteen directions without a break. The man was like an indiscriminate and unfocused motor-mouth. Anytime the other person would say something a little different, the talker would immediately shift to that subject and talk about himself relative to the new subject—where he had been, what he had done, etc.

Jim, who teaches communication skills to executives using his book, **So, What's Your Point?**, has his students conduct an interesting communication exercise. On an airplane, they are to ask the passenger next to them conversational questions, to find points of interest (e.g., career, hobbies, children, experiences) and let them talk all they want. The goal of the exercise is to see how long they can engage the stranger in talking about himself before he ever shows reciprocal interest. Personally, Jim has made this exercise last an entire flight. People have shared incredibly personal matters, yet at the end of the conversation, they don't even know Jim's name or occupation.

One of the greatest ways to show respect is to listen to the other person, to draw him out and to have him tell you who he is, what he does, what he is thinking and feeling, and what he is learning. But what if the other person doesn't reciprocate and never shows interest in you? If he never shows interest in you, why try to force it? Some men's egocentric nature prevents them from being candidates for high performance friendships. They could benefit from some personal coaching which, depending on our relationship with them, may or may not be appropriate to offer.

We have both come away from professional and social functions where we realized no one had asked us anything about what we do, how we decided on our careers, how we have impacted the lives of other people or been impacted by the people in our chosen fields. On the other hand, we have felt immense respect from and for people who have made us the priority for the few minutes we were able to talk to them at such gatherings.

John was at a social evening with old friends, and after a great deal of listening with hardly an opportunity to speak, he observed to a very close friend, "I have been listening to banter all night and noticed that no one has asked me any questions about what I do. Do you think it's because they know I am a pastor and it makes them uncomfortable? Maybe they fear I will preach to them." The friend responded, "I doubt it. I'm not a pastor, but no one asks me anything about my business or what I do, either. So, it is not about your faith. It is about people not caring and not showing respect."

As a Professor I Still Marvel at What I Heard – Jim

As a professor, I still marvel at the fact that John flunked out of college his sophomore year. It was not for lack of aptitude. I was impressed that John respected our friendship enough that he felt comfortable sharing what others would conceal, especially to a professor friend. When I asked him where he went after he flunked out of the University of Oregon, he said, "M.I.T."

That did not make sense, so I pressed. It turns out that there was a small private community college where lots of guys in John's situation went. It was Multnomah College in downtown Portland. So, the guys called it Multnomah in Town, or M.I.T., for short.

I'm originally from Massachusetts and worked with a think tank in Cambridge, right next to the real MIT. As a point of amusement, the Harvard faculty refers to the Massachusetts MIT as the vocational school down the street.

John made me laugh when he said the president had wanted to meet every new student. He took one look at John's transcript and said, "It must have been a good term down there [Eugene is one hundred miles to the south] because we have a lot of you boys up here this term."

In my career, I have given lots of bad grades but have not always had the opportunity to know what happened to those students. So

I asked John how his parents handled the bad news. He said, "My dad was great. He would laugh and kiddingly say, 'I got one smart kid and one dumb one.' (My brother was in medical school at the time.) It was total acceptance and by his humor he refused to let me get down on myself. He kept saying, 'What can I do to help you get back into Oregon?'"

As I listened to John, I realized his father was showing John immense respect and was focusing on his abilities to study and learn instead of his goofing off and getting thrown out of college.

My Friend Who Went to the Real MIT – John

Jim's parents moved to Minnesota to be close to the grandchildren. I loved them both immediately. They reminded me of a team—a salesperson and an inventor. Maggie was the salesperson, who was always smiling and talking and Mead was the inventor, who was always thinking. Mead never said much, but I always had the perception that there was a very fine computer whirling between his ears. I did not know he studied physics at the real MIT until Jim told me. Of course, I never told Mead that I got four Ds in high school physics either.

When you are a young pastor and helping to lead a growing and dynamic church, there are some people, old enough to be your parents, who continue to treat you as though you are a child. It is an act of great disrespect—instead of treating you with respect for the contribution you are making to a church and community, they ignore the words of the Apostle Paul when he says, "let no one look down on your youth." But Mead always treated me with respect and honored me as his pastor and the leader of the church. I never sensed him trying to play intellectual one-upmanship on me. Of course, that would not have been hard for him to do.

The Apostle Paul also said, "Treat an older man as you would your father." And that is how I endeavored to treat Mead—with the respect I hoped my father was getting from his own pastor, who was also young enough to be his son.

One night Mead and I were watching the Super Bowl together. I knew he had been involved in the development of the hydrogen bomb and asked him, "What was it like to sit in that bunker and see that bomb explode?" There was a long silence. Then a one-word answer that did not need to be a sentence or a paragraph: "Impressive!"

What a picture—the real MIT—the hydrogen bomb—and me. With four Ds in physics and M.I.T., all I ever felt and got from Mead was respect.

Mead could speak volumes with few words. When my father passed away, Mead and Maggie sent a sympathy card with a simple, compelling note that read, "We Care."

Respectfully Disagree – John

It was while I was at M.I.T. that I committed my life to Christ. When I returned to the University of Oregon, a number of Christian students and campus ministers helped me know more about being a follower of Christ. Also, I began to take religion courses to learn as much as I could about Christianity.

One of my professors was Dr. Alfred Bloom. Dr. Bloom was in the process of leaving the Christian faith and was on his way to becoming a Buddhist. He made me work hard; he made me think; he challenged my thinking, and he showed me respect.

Last year, while on vacation in Hawaii, I happened to read an article he wrote in the newspaper. I called the religion department at the University of Hawaii, from which he had retired. After retiring, he taught Buddhism at Berkeley for eight years and then returned to Hawaii. I had not seen him for forty-four years, but they agreed to forward an email to him.

We were able to meet for a late lunch on a Sunday afternoon. It was a delightful time and I got to meet his lovely wife, Dottie. He came from the Buddhist temple and she came from her Methodist church. I was able to tell Dottie how much her dear husband meant to me and how often I have referred to his influence in my life over the years of my ministry. It was a great time of reunion.

I am a follower of Christ and I make no apology for that. I was influenced early in my faith at Oregon by a brilliant professor who was leaving the Christian faith. Do I think he is wrong? Jesus said, "I am the way, the truth and the life and no one comes to the Father but through Me." That is the answer to the question. But that does not mean I have any right to be disrespectful. I have the greatest respect for Dr. Alfred Bloom. It was an utter delight to see him, and I plan to take Susan to meet Dottie and him when we return to Hawaii next year.

Showing Respect to Help Friends Grow – John

A number of men have told us they have felt disrespected by friends when the friends made a necessary correction. I was meeting with the board of one of the churches to which I was a consultant. The members were pretty rough on one another; kindness did not seem to be in the room. Finally, I said something to the men about how they were treating one another. One man, in an honest moment said, "This is nothing compared to how we treat one another where I work." I responded by asking, "Is how your co-workers treat each other relevant to how we treat each other here? Should we not treat each other the way Jesus said we should treat each other?" To his credit, the man was mature enough to accept the point.

If we respect someone, we want the best for them. Jesus said we are to love our neighbors as ourselves. Thus, we have to ask ourselves, are we simply commenting on behavior we do not like, or do we genuinely want to help our friends to improve. In other words, our motivation should be examined to ensure our efforts come from a place of respect.

I have seen relationships deteriorate in situations where guys make a federal case and embarrass a friend by abrasively correcting behavior as innocuous as golf protocol, driving directions or business theory. The motivation appears to be more promoting of one's own expertise than being helpful.

I know a well-regarded pastor who was visited by a mixed-race couple. They had asked for the appointment and told him they needed his advice. They explained they had a friend who said something they thought was racist. They did not know how to approach him. The pastor asked, "Is he the kind of person who wants to improve and be a better person?" They answered, "Yes." The pastor continued, "Then you should to talk to your friend." So, they said, "Okay, we are here and ready, if you are."

It was actually the pastor who they thought had said something racist. Their approach was absolutely respectful and kind. And, they were concerned about helping their pastor grow; they were not attempting to put him down.

Mutual respect is key to high performance friendships.

Christ's Approach to Respect

Sometimes, we think we can be friends only with those who are like-minded and who share many of the same likes and interests as our own. This was certainly not true with Jesus when He walked the earth. His friends/disciples were a very diverse group.

Luke (although not one of Jesus' disciples but a Gentile convert years later) was a logically thinking doctor, although we recognize he certainly would not qualify as a physician today; Peter was bombastic and impetuous; Thomas was cautious and analytical. After the word spread that Jesus was resurrected, Thomas was doubtful of the veracity of the rumor. He said he would not believe until he put his fingers in Jesus' wounds. One night, Jesus appeared to the group and said to Thomas, "Put your finger here; see My hands. Reach out your hand and put it into My side." Jesus knew who Thomas was. He did not berate him; He encouraged him; He showed him the truth.

The Apostle John helps us understand how Jesus treated people when He was on earth with this description: "He was full of grace and truth." In the Biblical sense, grace is God reaching out to us without asking anything in return—His love freely given. Simply stated, grace means to serve the purpose of making people better by helping them grow in whatever area of life they need to grow. Truth is truth without blemish. Jesus was always sincere, and never clouded any issue with smoke and mirrors. We think that Jesus was the Ultimate Respecter in how He treated others. No putdowns, no one-upmanship, no competition—just helping people be better through grace and truth.

Nicodemus was a Pharisee and a member of the Jewish ruling council. He was a well-respected and well-known Jewish leader and teacher of the Jewish religion. He came to Jesus one night and said to Him that people knew He was from God, for no one could do the miracles He was doing unless God was empowering Him to do so.

Jesus could have nailed Nicodemus for not being a follower, but He didn't. He treated him with respect. He did not deal with their differences—He dealt with the truth. He said to Nicodemus, "I am telling you the truth. No one can enter God's kingdom unless he be born again."

Nicodemus did not understand and asked if that meant somehow returning to the womb of his mother. Jesus did not mock him as a religious leader for not understanding this great truth. Again, He treated him with respect and spoke the truth to him. Jesus said,

"Very truly, I tell you, no one can enter the kingdom of God unless they are born of water and the Spirit. Flesh gives birth to flesh, but the Spirit gives birth to spirit. You should not be surprised at My saying, 'You must be born again.'" Because Jesus was truthful with him in a respectful manner, Nicodemus was motivated to become a follower of Jesus.

Another perspective on respect is to see it as caring and loving. The Apostle Paul writes of Jesus, "But God demonstrates His own love for us in this: While we were still sinners, Christ died for us." Jesus teaches us that respect is not given just because someone has accomplished something or won a championship or a coveted position. When we were sinners and "enemies of God," He pursued us. He reached out to us. He respected us and gave us the opportunity to approach Him.

The Apostle James adds weight to Jesus' admonition to love others as we love ourselves, and he helps us know how to respect people when he says, "Be quick to listen and slow to speak." Relative to the man on the airplane that John heard, James is saying we should be listening to others. When we listen, we are showing respect and love. Neither of us are psychologists but we wonder why some men always need to be talking. We have found guys talking as experts when they do not even know what they are talking about.

In Chapter 8, we talk about Jesus as our inner compass. By this we mean He is our standard for all we do. This means we slow down long enough to evaluate our lives against Him and how He lived. Since the Bible says, "be quick to listen and slow to speak," we should take the personal challenge of monitoring and evaluating ourselves.

Principles for Showing Respect to Friends

Respect is something we all desire; no one has ever said, "I hope my wife and children and my employees show me disrespect today." The Golden Rule implores us to treat others as we want to be treated. Since we all want to be treated respectfully, then it follows that we should be showing respect to others. This is tough, but it would behoove us to ask a close and honest friend, "Do I show respect to others? How? When? Where and when do I not show respect?" We all have a lot to learn in this area, and we will learn only as we allow others to speak to us honestly about our lives.

Showing respect can happen by being aware when we speak. Are people listening? Do we talk more than we listen? Do we consider—genuinely consider—what people say? Do we ask why they say it, or are we quick—very quick—to respond with what we assume is wisdom and the right answer?

Jesus said that after loving God, the second law is that we are to "love our neighbors as we love ourselves." Unless we are emotionally, spiritually or mentally imbalanced, we go to great lengths to love, nourish and cherish ourselves. Thus, it follows that a big part of respect is to nourish, cherish and care for our friends—and not to compete with them.

It is true that everyone is on a journey toward or away from God. When our lives intersect with others, how we treat them determines whether we can impact positively. If we do not treat others with respect, it's doubtful that we will impact them. Showing respect is not giving assent or agreement to someone else's views. Rather, showing respect to someone with whom we disagree is a manifestation of the humility that God showed us when we were not on a journey toward Him.

It has been said that "respect is commanded not demanded." This is true. However, the truly humble man tries to figure out how to show respect to everyone he meets. The college educated supervisor can give a compliment to the truck driver who has faithfully worked for the same company for thirty years. The rich factory owner can show respect to the factory worker who works every day and does not complain. Humility and respect go hand in hand. The humble man wants to show respect to everyone he meets because he was given a gift from God and he wants to give the gift to others.

Discussion Questions and Applications

1. Men often say that they hear from a third party how much they mean to someone or how well someone thinks they did on a particular assignment or project. Why is it that men seem to have such a hard time expressing respect directly to a person and kudos for a job well done?

2. What is more respectful: to express a concern or problem directly to the offender or talk to others about it? Why is that? What is the solution?

3. Is it possible that we men have been so inculcated by the competitive aspect of our culture that we think that to show another man respect by congratulating him somehow diminishes us?

4. We stated above that some men cannot seem to show respect when they offer corrections. Why is there such a competitive edge to what so many men say?

5. Consider your closest friendships. How often do you congratulate those friends or tell them they have done a good job? Do you ever belittle or minimize a friend's accomplishment, perhaps intending it to be in good fun? Is it awkward for some men to sincerely compliment or congratulate a friend? If so, why is that?

6. Starting today, how can we do a better job of showing respect to our friends? Think of a couple of friends, and think how you can show them more respect than you have up to this point.

7. What stories about respect can you share with your friends in a helpful manner?

Chapter 4

Intimacy

A friend is one before whom I may think aloud.
~ Ralph Waldo Emerson

Intimacy is a challenge for men in relationships, but it is pivotal to achieving high performance friendships. Some say the lack of intimacy comes from a fear of not seeming macho or of seeming feminine. But what is intimacy? Simply put, it means to be close to someone or others, while isolation means the separation from someone or others. Referencing Emerson's quote above, it means close enough to share our inner thoughts, feelings, dreams and fears.

The fact is that many men know a lot about their friends and yet know nothing at all. They do not know their friends' deepest secrets, fears, dreams and desires. It might be because: they are not interested; do not want to get that close; do not want to hear those kinds of inner thoughts; do not have relationships with those men who would share such things; and/or, they have friendships with men who don't or perhaps don't know how to share such intimate thoughts.

In Chapter 2 on Humility and Honesty, we (authors) shared our experiences with older guys abusing us (i.e., More Common than You Might Know stories). By sharing, we learned we both had similar experiences and were better able to put the experiences in perspective.

Dr. Kevin Meyer, in a private conversation with John, said, "We develop patterns of caring for and protecting ourselves—patterns that later become prisons that keep us from intimacy with Christ and others."

Ken Sande helps us understand that some men so idolize their way of thinking and their need to speak that they care little about listening to others. It is difficult to achieve intimacy with a person who is more concerned about what he thinks than any desire to listen to or understand another man's thoughts or feelings.

In **Uncommon Graces: Christ-Like Responses to A Hostile World** (Vawter, 1998), Dr. Ray Burwick, a friend and retired counselor shares this, "Some of the smartest people who come to see me are the best liars. They pay money to sit there for sixty minutes and lie." When asked why they would do that, he answered, "Because they don't want to face their own weaknesses."

How often do we hide a mistake or weakness and actually lie if asked? Have you ever observed the hypocrisy of men openly joking about a mistake or weakness of another when some within the group are in the same boat? Would we and our friends benefit more if we could be intimate enough to share our areas where we need growth and openly converse and encourage each other? Why are we so reluctant to reveal our hopes and fears? More importantly, what do we lose by not having intimacy in our friendships with men?

Let's consider some stories on intimacy and see what we can learn to help us achieve high performance friendship.

Illusion of Activities as Intimacy – John

First, I like to call myself a provincial berry picker from the east side of Portland, where I was raised. During my freshman year of college, I met some fascinating men living in the dormitory. Bill, whom I liked immediately, was from the Bay Area. He had grown up around the country club where his father was the golf professional. Bill was also on the university's varsity golf team. He had a level of sophistication about him that I had never seen in anyone else our age.

78

Over the years, I kept up with him through mutual friends. Then a couple of years ago, we were able to have lunch together. It was marvelous to reconnect with him. He was the same wonderful person as a grown man as when we met during the first few days of college at the age of eighteen.

During lunch, we talked about male friendships. Bill told me he had recently left the country club to which he had belonged for years. For the past fifteen years, he had played golf every week with the same guys; they had even traveled together on golf outings around the country and in other countries. Sadly, he said that from the day he left the club, he never got a telephone call from any of those men. Amazing! Fifteen years—and one day it is as though he had dropped off the planet. Apparently, he had been a golf pal, but not a friend with whom they could share. Was there no connection or intimacy beyond the activity of golf?

Professional Intimacy Gesture that Lasted a Lifetime – Jim

As a newly minted PhD and assistant professor at the University of Houston, I was challenged and anxious about the publish or perish world of academia. Dr. Jack Ivancevich was the most distinguished professor and researcher on the faculty. He was a big, powerful man who looked like he could have played power forward for the basketball team at the University of Kentucky, his alma mater.

My first week on the faculty, Jack called me into his office and said, "Please sit down. I want to show you something." He reached back to his credenza and grabbed a letter and a stack of papers. He continued, "You know, faculty egos are something else. Everyone around here is going to act like everything they submit gets published. Don't believe them."

To my astonishment, Jack shared, "I get rejected all the time." He then placed the stack of papers in front of me and said, "Look, here is a review of a recent submission." Jack went on to read off comments made by the editor and the reviewers, who are cloaked in anonymity. He agreed with a couple of comments and pointed out how another missed the point, etc. He was relaxed and sometimes chuckled at some of the comments that were off point. Most importantly, he generously exposed in an intimate way that the revered Jack Ivancevich had to take his licks and so would I—but it was OK. I was astonished but, importantly, impressed that Jack would share criticism so intimately and confidently. In reflection, it was Jack's intimacy with me that drew me to him and convinced me he was a man I could trust.

We served on the same faculty at Houston for only three years decades ago but that conversation was the beginning of a lifetime friendship. We collaborated in work often. Jack's gift of intimacy was one that I made a point of sharing with my doctoral students and junior colleagues. I had the opportunity to thank Jack for his gift many times before he passed away several years ago.

Jack's example taught me as a young man that intimacy is a compelling way to build friendship. But it requires transparency, confidence and humility. My friend taught me a wonderful lesson.

"Minnesota Nice" Should Include Hugs – John

When we lived in Minnesota, we often talked about "Minnesota nice," which means you never say a bad word or tell people how bad things are.

There is the fictitious story about the Minnesota farmer who had an accident on his tractor out in the field. He was able to crawl back to the house and his wife took him to the doctor. The doctor told him his leg would have to be amputated. His wife's response was, "Well, at least you didn't lose both of them."

Strangely, part of the reserve of Minnesota nice is to never overtly show affection to people. I didn't realize I was feeling very comfortable with that attitude until after my father died back in Oregon.

Maybe for the first time in my life, people other than family members hugged me.

I subconsciously adopted this new behavior. Sometime later, someone in the Minnesota church observed a marked difference in me upon my return from Dad's funeral. They pointed out that I was hugging people and putting my arm around them. Until it was called to my attention, I had not noticed the change.

What had happened? I had felt the power of touch from people who loved my father and expressed that love to me in a tangible and physical way. I saw the power of it and began to express the same, even though I did not know I was doing it.

Aware of the change, I now embrace hugs as an effective way to be intimate through touch and body language. A hug says a great deal about caring without words.

Pornography Alert – Jim

I was participating in an adult Bible study group with a leader I admire greatly. His knowledge of the Bible, his ability to teach and the example he set were inspiring.

In one of our lessons, he was talking about how research shows a common element in those who make major blunders in life, such as former President Richard Nixon with Watergate. The common element is that they don't have a good friend to hold them accountable and challenge their decisions.

As a point of interest, some years ago I was speaking on the same program as former news correspondent David Brinkley in Washington D. C. Since he had interacted with every US President since Harry Truman, during lunch I asked him his thoughts on them. His comment on President Nixon was enlightening. He said Nixon was the smartest President he had met but, due to being very paranoid, he was vulnerable to something like Watergate. Smart certainly doesn't keep us from making bad decisions.

Our class leader went on to explain that at one point he found himself becoming addicted to viewing pornography on the Internet. I was stunned. This man was practically a saint to me. First, I couldn't believe he would be susceptible to the temptation of pornography, and secondly, that he would share it with our group.

Talk about an intimate revelation! I never saw that coming. Had I heard it about him from someone else, I would not have believed it.

He went on to explain that for a man to think he is not susceptible to the sins of lust is for him to think he is more courageous than David, wiser than Solomon and stronger than Samson. His solution to his problem was to confide in a friend and ask the friend to challenge him periodically to make sure he had reverted from that behavior.

I consider a good lesson one that I never forget—and this was one of them. The courage of our group leader to share something so intimate and relevant was compelling. He was not a hypocrite, and his teaching by example was a generous gift of intimacy. He was so courageous and trusting that a lesser person in our group might have complained that our teacher wasn't worthy. There was nothing but admiration for him.

From his example, I learned that openly admitting our struggles with temptations allows us to be more accessible and, ironically, more credible with our friends. If we pretend to be better (perfect?) than we are, it makes it more difficult for our friends to come to us when they have challenges and weaknesses.

Death, a Time for Intimacy – John

Ministers are often called upon to deal with the loss of loved ones, which should provide a defining opportunity for intimacy. Women fare better than men during these times.

In my fourteen years of pastoring in Minnesota, I officiated at the memorial services for fourteen children—from still-born to young adult. All of them were difficult assignments and took something out of me I do not think I have ever regained.

One of the most painful was the experience of an outstanding young man who had committed suicide. I was close to the family beyond the normal pastor/parishioner relationship. In fact, I broke down and wept during the service because of the pain and loss I was feeling.

The young man's parents have remained close friends. Reuel Nygaard, the father, told me that men would call and, after brief condolences, say that the wives should talk. It was in those conversations that the caller's wife would say to the grieving mother, "My husband wants to know how your Reuel is doing?"

Amazing! The two men had just talked, and yet the caller let his wife ask the grieving mother how the grieving father was doing, thereby avoiding intimate conversation that should happen between men who are friends.

As a courtesy, I asked Reuel if it was all right to use this story in the book. After granting permission, he added a new insight. He said, "On occasion, men would ask me how my wife was, and I wanted to yell at them, 'How about me? Why don't you ask how I am?'"

He went on to say, "I hope your book will help men be more sensitive to being open and honest. I know that my transparency has opened the door for other men to share with me." Reuel went on to say that after his son died, a close friend of eighteen years asked to see him. The man told Reuel that his father was a butcher and an alcoholic. One night, the mother was washing his father's blood-stained work clothes with a flammable detergent when his intoxicated father walked in the door and, in his stupor, threw a lit match at his wife. Reuel's friend, then just a boy, watched his mother burn to death.

Reuel continued, "It took my son's tragedy for my friend to open up and tell me this secret." When we are transparent, people feel safe. In his transparency, he has written a great book about suicide, **From Tragedy to Triumph**.

As a second story, Paul was a pastor in Minnesota, and also a mentor and dear friend to me. I grieved when he moved to Connecticut. I never saw him alive again. Shortly after moving, he contracted pancreatic cancer. I called him as often as was proper. When he was near death, I remember saying to him, "Paul, this is really serious. How are you doing?" After telling me how he was doing and telling me how he felt about being so close to death, he said something that really shocked me. He said, "John, lots of friends have called, but you are the first one to ask me how I feel about dying. I appreciate that." When I asked him what those callers had talked about, he said, "Generalities."

And then there was the bizarre time when my highly exaggerated obituary was published by mistake. My brother, Mike, and I were members of the same fraternity in college but in different years. A couple of years ago, I was erroneously declared dead by the national office of the fraternity. I was told later that a man in the fraternity, who was of Mike's era and very close to him, was asked if he was going to call to express condolences over my death. The man said he was not going to call because he did not want to make Mike sad. That lack of intimacy still boggles my mind. How can you not call a friend of over 40 years to express condolences when you have heard that the man's younger brother has died?

Parenthetically, there is the famous Irish joke that applies: Gallagher opened the morning newspaper and was dumbfounded to read in the obituary column that he had died. He quickly phoned his best friend, Finney. "Did you see the paper?" asked Gallagher. "They say I died!!" "Yes, I saw it!" replied Finney. "Where are ye callin' from?" When I called the national office to report that I was still alive, the man did not ask where I was calling from nor did he apologize. However, he did have the guts to ask for a donation to the organization. So much for intimacy.

It is sad and hard to explain why men tend to avoid intimacy. Offering intimacy can be such a meaningful gesture to a friend and can lead to high performance friendship.

Intimacy in an Instant – Jim

Having suddenly lost my best friend, Jim Evans, when we were eighteen, I have always been highly sensitive to the loss of loved ones.

There was a tragic news story of twin sisters, Kayla and Kelsey, who were on their way home from high school when an out-of-control dump truck collided with their car. Kelsey lost her life and Kayla suffered minor injuries. I didn't know it at the time, but Kelsey, like my friend Jim, was well prepared to meet her Maker; Kayla was still struggling with her faith, as was their father Thom, a school superintendent who was not unfamiliar with parents losing children.

I have a practice of sending my book, **Faith Logic**, to parents who lose their children. I had never met Thom but felt moved to send him the book, as Chapter 4 provides what book reviewers consider an insightful and comforting perspective on death. I resisted the initial hesitation I often feel before making this gesture, as I don't want to presume anything about anyone's faith. I always explain my loss as part of the gift, in hopes of properly explaining my reason for offering it.

A few months later, Thom called and thanked me for sending the book and asked if we could meet for lunch. We did. Without any pretense, we instantly connected and conversed intimately.

After sharing the excruciating pain of having lost his daughter Kelsey, we talked about God. Thom was baptized at fourteen in Iowa but confided he had just been going through the motions and soon had doubts that peaked when he was a graduate student in psychology. He developed a friendship with a fellow student who turned out to be gay. He said the friend was a wonderful person,and Thom could not reconcile his church's rejection of gay people. He felt it was hypocritical to be a friend and still attend that church. He felt disconnected from God, the Bible and church.

He never gave up pursuing life's biggest question. As with me, having children is a strong motivator to get answers. Books like **Mere Christianity** by C. S Lewis and **More than a Carpenter** by Josh McDowell increased his understanding, as they have mine.

At 52, two years before Kelsey died, Thom became a Christian. It was not an "on the road to Damascus" conversion like the Apostle Paul. Rather, it was more gradual, with starts and stops. It was not as deep then as it is now.

In contrast, I became a Christian and was baptized at six years old, but an unchallenged faith got seriously derailed in college, and I spent many miserable years where doubt prevailed over faith. I also discovered that not believing allowed me to live my life as I chose—which had painful consequences.

I experienced the same starts and stops on my journey of galvaniz-ing my faith. It was a long journey for both of us and Thom and I agreed God had incredible patience. We both had similarly shared more of an intellectual faith before coming to the too-good-to-be-true faith when the amazing beauty of grace is comprehended.

He went on to explain that Kelsey was such a strong Christian: "The best of us." he said, referring to his family. He felt moved by her example and recommitted his life to God, which took his faith to a whole new level. He shared how my book had helped with his faith. I later learned other books that had been helpful included Young's **The Shack**, another gift from a stranger.

Thom, of course, knew of my faith struggles from **Faith Logic** as it is written for the strong-willed and spiritually challenged. I sympathized with him about his church conflict resulting from his gay friend. I shared with him that a close family member of mine is gay and that God's love for me and my love of God enhances my love for her.

The church I attend accepts that or it would not be my church.

Thom explained he was going to be baptized again as a recommitment of his life to Christ. I asked if I could attend with my wife, Brynn. He said he would be honored. It was special to be there and watch the water ease pain as it streamed from Thom's face. We, as others, could feel the presence of the Holy Spirit in the room.

A few months later, Thom called me and said he was inspired to write a book about the tragedy and faith with Kelsey's boyfriend, John Michael (JM), who was the love of her life. He wanted to know if I would meet with them and offer guidance on book writing. Thom told me he had learned that I had donated copies of **Faith Logic** to the fund raiser for Kelsey's memorial garden at the high school, and he was thankful. Funds were also raised for an ongoing scholarship in Kelsey's name.

We met and had a wonderful conversation. JM is a handsome young man whose faith is as beautiful as Kelsey's. I offered as many suggestions and as much encouragement as possible.

A year later, John and I had just completed writing this book when I received Thom's book, **Tragedy and Trust**, in the mail. It is a wonderful book, written as only two men who were so hurt and loved so well could write. As a result, I knew I had one more story to add to my own book, and I now also had another book to encourage you to read.

There is a particularly moving aspect of the story, explained in Thom's book, when a nurse mistakenly caused confusion as to which of the sisters had died:

For that split second, he (John Michael) felt relieved, but then he thought of Todd (Kayla's boyfriend), of how Kelsey would take losing her sister, and pain stabbed him again. He thought of how much Kelsey cared for Kayla, and how they had both prayed for Kayla to come into her own intimate relationship with the Lord. Then he knew, if anyone had to die, it had to be Kelsey—Kelsey had the stronger faith.

What is so profound is that it is the same feeling that my friends and I felt about our friend, Jim Evans, when he died. He, as Kelsey, was ready—he had the strongest faith.

Thom kindly enclosed the following note in my copy of his book:

Jim and Brynn, Thank you so much for all that you have done for me and my family—for the books that we sold, for the advice on the manuscript, for your friendship. God Bless. Thom.

I called to thank Thom and to celebrate his book. I couldn't believe how joyful he sounded compared to when we had last spoken. He told me how God moves his life forward with new wonderful chapters. I was especially moved when he told me of how the pictures of Kelsey around the house used to be painful reminders of loss— pictures of pain he called them. Now he and his family see Kelsey as a gift of eighteen years that they will spend eternity with when the time comes.

And to think, for a moment I hesitated to send a book to a man I did not know and would not have known as a friend. Intimacy provides the close connection for high performance friendship.

Christ's Approach to Intimacy

As stated above, some men consider being emotionally intimate with other men as being unmasculine. This simply is not true, unless Jesus was less than masculine—which we do not think He was—when He wept over the death of His friend, Lazarus, or when He was grieving in the Garden of Gethsemane as He was agonizing over what He would endure to be crucified for the sins of the world.

When Jesus gathered His disciples in Jerusalem for the Last Supper to give them their final marching orders, He did not leave the discussion at the orders stage. Rather, He told them they were entering an entirely new relationship with Him where He was no longer going to call them servants, but was going to call them friends and reveal to them everything the Father revealed to Him.

His explanation to the disciples about what this revelation to them meant is absolutely fundamental to our understanding of why Jesus is the model for male friendships. He is not talking about doing things together; He is not talking about how the Bethlehem Badgers are going to do in the Super Bowl; rather He is talking about the most intimate and painful issues of His life as the Savior of the world. He explains in detail what that means.

We think His explanation and His intimacy can and do help us evaluate whether we are genuinely friends by His standard or simply people who care for one another and enjoy being together. Intimate friendship is deep level friendship.

After Jesus finished giving the disciples their final marching orders in the upper room and after He prayed, He went out to the Garden of Gethsemane. He allowed Peter, James and John to be close enough to know what was going on. He said to them, "I am extremely sorrowful, even to the point of death. Stay here and comfort Me. Pray so that you will not be tempted." Jesus was in agony. He sweated drops of blood; He tried to bargain with God to find another way to deal with the forgiveness of sin for mankind.

How do we know this? He let the three men be close enough to hear. Jesus was honest with His followers; He was honest with Himself; He was honest with God.

We believe Jesus is talking about a relationship that we doubt any of us understands. We say this because in His perfection He was not selfish, was never on an ego trip, never needed to put others down and always told the truth. We believe His words to His friends and how He treated His friends should motivate all of us who are serious about deepening our friendships to ask ourselves just how much we share with our friends and how much they share with us—and at what level.

Principles for Intimacy in Friendship

From the stories in this chapter and examples provided by Christ, we develop an understanding of intimacy and friendship that includes being open and vulnerable, not hiding fears, dreams and weaknesses. It means having immense trust that someone keeps private the things we share with him.

If we consider Christ's example, He honored His friends and did not keep secrets from them. He was willing to share His emotions and His deepest concerns. Why should we be reluctant to be equally intimate with our friends?

Because intimacy is encouraged by Christ's example, it should be no surprise that it is good for us. Professor Matthias Mehl, of the University of Arizona, reports that people who have deeper conversations report being the happiest. Happy people engage in about twice as many substantive conversations and engage in only about a third as much trivial small talk as the unhappiest people (*Psychology Science*, 2010).

Trust, of course, as discussed in Chapter 6, is an important variable in intimacy. Intimacy includes a protective spirit over things spoken in private. For example, couples in love do not share their intimacies freely with others—that is the dynamic of intimacy. As Tournier says in **Secrets** (1966), if we share everything without discretion, we are not human because God means for us to have discernment among our relationships. Conversely, if we share nothing, we are not human because God means for us to rely on and share with one another.

Unfortunately, some people confuse gossip with intimacy. There are men who incorrectly think it is intimate to share their sexual conquests. Gossiping/bragging exposes the person who is not there to defend himself. Frankly, it is taking advantage of him. As a minister, John has been surprised over the years by how many men have felt the need to share their experiences with him. It makes no sense. It may reveal a lack of self-esteem or a profound insecurity to talk in such a way that does such damage to people— it is certainly not intimacy.

Intimacy should uplift, not damage.

Honesty is key to intimacy. Pat Boris, in talking about the drug addict lying to himself, says, "The first lie is to God, by saying, 'I found something that works better than You do' and then the second lie is to yourself." Boris helps us understand a profound truth, regardless of what the issue is. If we are lying to God (which is useless because He knows our thoughts anyway), we will be lying to ourselves. So the man who refuses to let his friends get close to him is keeping God at a distance, too, **Hit by a Ton of Bricks: You're Not Alone When Your Child's on Drugs** (Vawter, 2011).

Intimacy is not static; it grows. A good example of this is our relationships with our wives. After years of marriage, we are still growing in our intimacy, sharing on a deeper and more profound level every year. We are not suggesting that all male friendships have a perfect state of intimacy because intimacy grows and develops. But we are making the point that many men do not have any level of intimacy in their friendships.

There is a dynamic of which we must be aware. Some might think that another person is not capable of intimacy when it might not be that at all. It might simply be that the person doesn't share because of a lack of trust. Some people are so intimidating that their soft criticisms can feel like an attack, and recipients have the inner response, "I am not going to let you near me, and I am not going to listen to you."

Richard Hendrix makes an insightful comment and asks a tough question. He says one of King David's attributes was the humility to hear criticism. It is hard to be friends with someone who can never take advice, hear criticism or hear another perspective. Do we keep our friends at a distance because we resent their honesty? Or do we draw friends closer because they know it is always safe to be real with us?

We have observed four hindrances to intimacy in male friendships:

1) belligerent and argumentative—Some men simply refuse to be corrected or even consider they might be able to improve on something they are doing. Often, the response is being belligerent and argumentative rather than considering what their friend has to say.

2) always correct/subtle arrogance—Some men always have to be right-regardless of the subject (the foremost authority syndrome). When you are with someone who always has a quick answer and seems to have no interest in what others are thinking, you realize after awhile that there is no possibility of an intimate relationship with him.

3) passive aggressive—Some men are deflective and refuse to talk about anything of significance. They are very skillful at avoiding any talk that would get close to their deepest emotion or allow anyone to get close to them.

4) shop talk—For some men, the extent of their conversation is professional or ministerial shop talk, primarily about their work or hobbies. They seem incapable of talking about love for their wives or kids, their fears for the future or what is on the inside. It is hard to be intimate with such people.

In summary, intimacy in friendship requires:

- being open and vulnerable
- not hiding fears, dreams and weaknesses
- having immense trust that a friend keeps private the things we share with him

The undertone of this definition connotes growing, maturing and becoming more like Christ. If part of friendship at the deepest level is to help one another grow, there has to be a level of intimacy to let others make comments on our lives as well as let us make comments on theirs.

We need to remember we can never start an argument by listening to a friend.

Discussion Questions and Applications

1. Intimacy is described as "being open and vulnerable, not hiding fears, dreams or weaknesses and having an immense trust that a friend keeps private the things we share with him." Why do you think many men have such trouble achieving intimate friendships with other men?

2. Jesus did not have a problem being intimate and sharing His inner thoughts, feelings and emotions with others. Why do you think this is?

3. With how many men would you say you have an intimate friendship?

4. If we lack intimate male friendships and want to remedy the situation, what steps could we take?

5. How can you help the men in your life become more intimate in their friendships with other men?

6. What does this whole issue of intimacy teach us about Jesus Christ?

7. If you have a broken relationship, can you try to repair it with an intimate approach? Consider something like, "I value our relationship but fear it has been damaged. Do you miss the friendship we used to share? Could you tell me what I have done to contribute to the situation and what I can do to make it right?"

8. Are you comfortable having faith discussions with friends? Is that a possibility for deepening relationships? Perhaps you could start by asking a friend to share his faith story and, after listening carefully, consider if sharing yours might contribute to the conversation.

9. What stories about intimacy can you share in a helpful manner with your friends?

Chapter 5

Support

It's the friends you can call up at 4 a.m. that matter.
~ Marlene Dietrich

A friend is one who knows you as you are, understands where you have been, accepts who you have become and still gently invites you to grow.
~ William Shakespeare

Support is one of the great gifts and essentials of high performance friendship. To support a friend is to serve as his foundation. It is to uphold and sustain under trial or affliction with patience and tolerance.

True friends are ones I would call on—those on whom I would not be imposing. Who would call me first?

Men enjoy being known as Mr. Fix It. We like the sense of being in charge or control when there is a problem. Asking for help is often much more difficult for us. As we began to write this chapter on Support, we recalled the compelling lyrics written and sung by Bill Withers in the song, *Lean on Me*, and an interesting incident pertaining to the song and us. Withers' lyrics say it better and more poetically than we can, and they point out that support is a two-way street. Here they are for your consideration:

Sometimes in our lives, we all have pain
We all have sorrow
But if we are wise
We know that there is always tomorrow
Lean on me, when you're not strong
And I'll be your friend
I'll help you carry on
For it won't be long

Till I'm gonna need
Somebody to lean on.

Please swallow your pride
If I have things you need to borrow
For no one can fill those of your needs
That you don't let show.

Just call on me brother, when you need a hand
We all need somebody to lean on
I just might have a problem that you'll understand
We all need somebody to lean on

If there is a load you have to bear
That you can't carry
I'm right up the road I'll share your load
If you just call me

Call me (If you need a friend)
Call me (Call me)
Call me (If you need a friend)
Call me (If you ever need a friend)
Call me (Call me)
Call me
Call me (if you need a friend).

Songfacts shares Bill Withers' thoughts on the lyrics. He explains that, as he was playing with some simple piano progressions, the phrase *Lean on Me* emerged and he liked it. So he asked himself, "How do I arrive at this as a conclusion to a statement? What would I say that would cause me to say 'Lean on Me'? At that point, it's between you and your actual feelings, you and your morals and what you're really like."

Years ago, we were remodeling the church where John was pastor. The auditorium and its sound system were unavailable. John knew I was a rock musician as a teenager and that I kept a fully equipped bandstand in my home. He asked if I could bring my equipment, organize a group and provide music in the auxiliary room for a service.

His mistake was that he also told me he would have to be out of town. When he returned, he was curious about what song I had performed. I responded, "Lean on Me by Bill Withers." John looked puzzled and said, "It's a great song, but it's a secular song."

"Not to worry," I explained, "I took poetic license and added one more verse and repeated the chorus to make it legit." With apologies to Mr. Withers, I added:

> *God said feed my sheep*
> *If you love me*
> *Then my commandments keep*
> *Do unto others, as you would have them do unto you*
> *Just call on me brother.*

John smiled; little did he know he had just been given some interesting material for Chapter 6 on Trust for a book that we would co-author in a couple of decades.

Here are a few stories about support for your consideration.

The Worst News Ever – John

Because of how alcohol ravaged three of my uncles, I have never been interested in it. People cannot believe I lived in a fraternity in college (except when I was at M.I.T.) and had only two beers. I simply stayed away from it. I preached abstinence to our kids from the time they could understand. I told them they were playing Russian roulette if they chose to drink because I believe addiction is both a genetic imprint and a learned behavior. It is possible they have the gene.

So you can imagine my shock when Susan and I received a phone call telling us that one of our kids away at college had become addicted to heroin. The shock was so great that I could not breathe. Even though I am a minister, all I could pray as I held Susan was, "God, can you help us?"

It was absolutely the worst of times. I was devastated. I was also angry at God for a while—which is a very common response. I said, "I have given my life since college to serve You, and You let this happen to me!" In retrospect, I see that as a very, very selfish attitude. I was not thinking of my child or the effects of this news on Susan. I had the perception that I was a people helper; people came to hear my sermons, and they came to ask my advice. When they did not know where to turn, either other pastors in the church or I were there to help them. Now, I needed help.

Of course, Susan and I saw a professional, and we went to a support group (Nar Anon) for family members of addicts. But of even greater importance was the help and support I received from friends. I put these friends in two categories:

1. Friends who had walked the addiction road before me
2. Friends who had no idea what I was experiencing but proved they cared by listening and not offering advice

The first category of friends helped Susan and me accept that this addiction was not a result of our bad parenting skills. They helped us find a new trust in and reliance on God. I can remember one of them saying, "He is God and I am not!" None of these friends ever pried. They did not focus on the past; they focused on the future and what it could become—both for our child and for us. They talked frankly and directly about the stress that the addiction brought into their marriages. Some of them talked about the pain of having their kids on the streets or in jail. Their very demeanor convinced us they had survived, and that we would survive. Their faith in God convinced us we needed to deepen our faith in Him and we did. Their marital growth convinced us we needed to draw closer together and we did. Indeed, somewhere along the way, Susan and I picked up the little mantra, "I am not the enemy, darling." Sometimes out of my pain, I would hurl at Susan—the one I love the most. Or, she would hurl at me out of her pain. Instead of hurling back, we both realized from where the hurling came, and the words, "I am not the enemy, darling" was a soft way of saying, "You have gone over the edge. Let me help you back."

The second category of friends did not understand (how could they?), but they were great supporters. They let us talk; they did not interrupt. They did not give advice. They did not judge us as bad parents; indeed, they, too, said we had been good parents. Dr. James Kok's book title, **90% of Helping is Just Showing Up**, says it all. That is exactly what these friends did—they showed up.

Words I saw hanging on a wall in a restaurant many years ago embodied both categories of friends: A true friend walks in when the rest of the world walks out. This helped me understand that supportive friends have a goal in mind. It could be to help us develop a deeper faith in God; it could be to help us mature; it could be to help us think clearly once again. They might not state the goal but they have it.

When I think of support I think of some word pictures: a beam holding up a brick wall that has just been laid; a support staff helping an executive or the support staff in a political campaign. In each word picture, there is an end in mind—a new building, a good profit margin or a successful election. That is what these friends did for me. They had a goal in mind: for me to get healthy, for me to know I was not alone; and to let me know I was not disqualified from ministry because of a poor choice on the part of my wonderful child.

Sadly, some others tried to pry. They tried to figure out what Susan and I had done wrong. Frankly, I did not sense love and compassion from them. I sensed judgment. I found myself getting angry at them, their questions and prying. So I absented myself from them. I gave them non-answers when I could not avoid them. The Bible is clear that we are to flee from temptation. Since I could not avoid getting angry at them and I was afraid of giving them a piece of my mind that I really could not afford to lose, I absented myself. I have never regretted doing that. Indeed, I advise others in the same situation to do likewise.

Thankfully, our story turns out well. Many years later, our child is now a social worker working with teenage delinquent girls and teenage boys who have sexually molested other children. Currently, she is studying for her Masters degree in psychology to become an addiction counselor. Out of our pain has come a ministry—*You're Not Alone (www.notalone.org)*—to help other parents with kids who are abusing or addicted, and a book, **Hit by a Ton of Bricks** (Westbow, 2011). And out of respect for my daughter, she has read and approved everything I have told here. If she had not given permission, I would not have told the story.

Bailed Out in Boston – Jim

It has been said that criminal courts make good people out of bad people and civil courts make bad people out of good people. If you have ever been involved in civil litigation, you learn that it usually has less to do with truth and right than you would hope. It usually has more to do with spending money to force your opponent to spend more money, and whoever comes to their senses first loses. I don't even do expert witness work anymore because I find the process so distasteful.

I have prevailed in civil courts, but my legal fees often exceed what it would have cost just to settle. Why would I do that? One reason is that I am a professor, and we tend to be principled to a fault. I have been told by defense attorneys that they avoid professors for jury selection for just that reason. Jurors are persuaded by emotion or logic—emotion works best. But professors have a logic bias that can hang a jury that is otherwise persuaded.

I was involved in litigation as a defendant in a civil suit. I had a huge logistics and expense disadvantage because I had to repeatedly travel two thousand miles to Boston, rent a car and stay in a hotel in order to defend myself. The opposing attorney and the plaintiff were going to use all the predictable tactics to drive up my expenses. Tactics included not responding to discovery, thereby forcing me to incur the expense of a motion to compel discovery, then providing discovery that was not responsive, forcing the cycle to start over. They would repeatedly ask for continuances to play havoc with my work schedule. Once, after I traveled all the way to Boston to take a deposition, the plaintiff failed to show up, claiming forgetfulness. After I headed back to Logan airport, my attorney told me he spotted the plaintiff outside the building. I was out the time and expense—another exercise in frustration.

What made it possible to endure all of this nonsense and expense? A friend.

When the lawsuit was filed, I knew I was in for a nuisance lawsuit that would be an attempt to inconvenience me into an unfair settlement. As an author and consultant, I was busy traveling extensively, speaking and consulting. It occurred to me to call a friend I had worked with when I was with a think tank consulting group in Boston. We really weren't more than cordial friends at the time, but I reached out nonetheless.

Bob was awesome. He said, "I know how stressful litigation can be. Jim, you are welcome to stay in our guest room whenever you come to town. As you know, Boston is a confusing city to navigate, the courthouse is fifty miles from Boston and difficult to find. Don't rent a car for your first trip; let me pick you up at the airport and take you to the courthouse."

Bob was there for me every step of the way. It was actually hard for me to take such generous support from a friend. I was usually on the giving side, as that was a more comfortable, manly position for me. The best part was the evenings Bob and I spent together sharing our thoughts and feelings. He would have been a great psychologist.

I was able to engage Bob as a consultant with a start-up company as result of our time together. When the company sold his stock, he received sufficient income to completely remodel his kitchen, family room and dining room and buy a new car for his wife, Cathy, who was so hospitable through the two years of litigation. But I felt that even Bob's good fortune paled in comparison to what he had done to support me.

As for the litigation, after two years, the opposition was able to force a schedule complication that would have ruined spending time with my daughters during their short time at home from college. I settled for one and a half cents on the dollar to avoid another round of nonsense. Attorneys will tell you it was a win, but it didn't feel like it.

The real win was developing a deep friendship with Bob, and, of course, Cathy. It is humbling and instructive to be on the receiving end of a friendship from a friend who is supportive because that is who he is.

I Could Use Some Toilet Paper – John

As Jim and I worked on this chapter, I called a dear friend of mine. He was there for me when drugs invaded our home. He was one of the first people I called, and he took me out for dinner so we could talk. When his son committed suicide, I was one of the first people he called, and I had taken him out for dinner so we could talk. I gave him a copy of Reuel Nygaard's book, mentioned in Chapter 4. As you can tell, we have walked a lot of rough roads together. We have not held back any secrets and have shown genuine dependence on each another.

The reason I called my friend is because he walks with crutches—the victim of a fairly simple but botched hip surgery; it might be a case for a malpractice lawsuit. He is walking worse today than after the surgery three months ago. His mobility is limited. And his wife had to leave town, due to a medical emergency with her parents.

I called to ask if he needed anything—was there anything I could do for him? There was a pause, and he said, "I could use some toilet paper." My mind raced as I pondered the scene, and I asked, "Right now?" thinking of the worst predicament. I was relieved when he said, "No, later in the day." When I delivered the paper a few hours later with a few other things he had requested from the store, he said, as I put the things down on the kitchen counter, "You do not know how difficult it was for me to have to ask for help."

Isn't that interesting? We have shared so much, carried each other, listened to each other and helped each other when we learned of drugs and suicide, and yet it was difficult to ask for toilet paper, soup and some other food items.

But that is what friends do: they walk in when the rest of the world walks out. The words to the song are so true, "He ain't heavy, he's my brother." On the wall in the cafeteria where my kids went to junior high school were these words: Friendship is a bunch of: effort, love, work, care and hope. Those words say it all...friendship is not always easy. But if we have a goal in mind—and I think the most important goal is helping one another become more Christ-like—it is worth the effort.

Someone said it this way: "Supporting a friend has the connotation of needing help, of having a goal, of getting somewhere and working for the same objective which is huge and compelling." As I have pondered these words, I have realized their depth. None of us is perfect. All of us need to take the next step in growth, whether it be spiritual, mental, emotional or physical growth. And the best way to get there is with the help of supportive friends.

Supportive Friends Tell the Truth – John

Many men I know speak of strong-willed friends who do not listen well. One in particular says many of his friends think they are always right, regardless of the topic or the truth. They can be aggressive and rude as they belligerently argue their points of view One man's wife calls his buddies of this ilk The Bulls when she discusses them with her husband. She says she would not want to be married to any of them, but she loves them nevertheless. She does not rationalize their rude and selfish behavior, but she understands who they are and wishes they could become better people.

She does not make excuses for them. She is aware of their lack of spiritual maturity and their refusal to bend their knee to Christ. Interestingly, the key word is rationalize—she does not rationalize for them.

Over the years, I have seen and heard some very interesting rationalizations for misconduct:

- That's just the way he is
- No one is perfect
- He was a whole lot worse before he became a Christian
- Give him a break
- He's had a tough life

Rather than being truthfully supportive and helping friends improve, men find it is easier to speak such clichés—even though that is not genuine friendship.

Compare all of these rationalizations with what one supportive but honest man said to his friend, a man who is notorious for being late and is always making excuses for his tardiness. The man was late arriving home, having frittered away the time. Unfortunately, when he arrived, his wife let him know in an unhappy and unkind way. His response was to lie and blame the slow clerk in the store where he had stopped on the way home.

Fortunately for him, his friend was with him and heard the outburst. Later, when they were alone, the supportive friend asked him why he had lied to his wife. It was not an easy conversation, but one that was needed. The man had developed a bad and irresponsible attitude about keeping his word relative to time, even lying about why he was late. His friend loved him too much to let him get away with it. He did not rationalize for the man, excusing him because he was busy and amiable. His amiability meant he did not want to say "no" to anyone who wanted to spend time with him, even if it meant someone on the other end had to wait.

The fallacy of that logic, however, is that the person on the other end of the equation—the one who is being kept waiting because the man is late—is indeed being told "no." And the man is developing a reputation that he is not dependable. So I believe that the friend who talked to this man had his very best interests at heart; he was and is a genuine friend and showed support by telling his friend the truth. He had a goal in mind—helping his friend be more responsible and be more truthful.

More Support Than I Could Accept – Jim

When I was an Associate Professor at the University of Minnesota, I was approached by another university offering a position as a Full Professor with an endowed chair. I was incredibly happy where I was, as our Management Information Systems (MIS) group was ranked as the top in the world. I was adjusting to my good fortune in having been recruited there from the University of Houston a couple of years earlier to be the Director of the MIS Research Center at Minnesota.

Nonetheless, this seemed like an opportunity to seek an early promotion to Full Professor at Minnesota, even though it was a bit treacherous. I had gone from Assistant to Associate in three years instead of the typical seven. Now I was going up for promotion to Full Professor in three years instead of the minimum guideline of five years.

There were two key people who had to support this move for me to have a chance. One was Gordon Davis, who is generally regarded as the Father of the field of MIS, as had he created the first MIS program at Minnesota and had written what is considered the defining book in the field, as well as other significant books and articles. The other person was a very distinguished professor, who will remain unnamed. Both agreed I had the teaching and research record to support an early promotion, and if I stayed at Minnesota, they would take the lead to support the promotion the next year.

The following year, Gordon, as promised, supported the promotion. To my brutal disappointment, the other professor did not. I was embarrassed, as the rest of the faculty would know I should have secured the support of both senior MIS faculty members to achieve an early promotion. Although I received a positive vote, it was marginal due to the split between the two senior faculty leaders. Without strong support, the possibility of early promotion was futile.

I had lost the opportunity for the full professorship offered the prior year, but fortunately another university was recruiting me in the midst of this awkward fiasco. So, I told Gordon I was leaving to take the new opportunity. Gordon kindly asked me not to leave and reminded me that we had no way to anticipate the other professor would not have kept his word. He said, "Stick around, we will get the promotion done next year because we will be prepared."

I thanked Gordon but explained that the only way I could save face was to accept the new offer as a Full Professor at the other university to prove I was worthy. (Yes, I can be that shallow!)

What Gordon said next is still astonishing: "Jim, don't leave; it would be a mistake for you and Minnesota. We can get this done next year. In fact if you are not promoted next year, you choose a different university, and I will go there with you." That was more support than I deserved or could accept. I was honored and grateful, though I told him I could not accept his gesture. What a friend!

Gordon is one of the most honorable men I know—and a great man of faith. He fixed the problem without waiting a year by taking the unprecedented step of talking to each faculty member individually and explaining what had happened. He told me he wanted everyone to know that the University would lose a valued colleague if corrective action were not taken now. He persuaded the faculty to call for another vote (never done before), where there was full disclosure as to why the two senior MIS faculty did not both support early promotion. This time, the vote was unanimous, except for two people—you can guess one, and the other one doesn't matter. Early promotion was granted and I served another eighteen years on the faculty at the University of Minnesota because of the support of a dear friend.

Gordon and I were not just supportive as professional friends— some of our best conversations focused on faith and sharing our experiences and points of view. A few years ago, Gordon was honored at a national recognition dinner, as he was retiring and shifting to Emeritus status. I was asked to deliver a keynote speech in his honor. Guess what story was a highlight of that keynote address? Even though Gordon didn't have to deliver on his astonishing offer, nor would I have let him, I learned an invaluable lesson about the power of support for a friend and the compelling bonding that results.

High performance friendships are supportive friendships.

Christ's Approach to Support

Because Jesus is not only the Savior of the world but also our teacher and model for life, we can learn volumes from Him as we observe how He lived and interacted with people. As it relates to the issue of supporting and being supported by friends, probably no part of His life speaks more clearly than His last few days and hours. Obviously, Jesus had faith. He relied on the Father. He would draw away from the crowds to re-energize Himself by being alone with the Father. But there was the human element as well. Simply stated, He relied on His friends, too.

When Jesus was giving His men their final marching orders in the Upper Room in Jerusalem, He made a tremendous statement about support. Support helps friends get better. Support helps friends become more like Christ. Jesus knew His men could not do what He was asking them to do—tell His message so a movement would start with the goal of taking it to the entire world—under their own power. So He promised them it was to their advantage that He go away. He said He would send the Comforter (the Holy Spirit) to guide and teach them.

Later, we understand that another responsibility of the Holy Spirit is to shape Christ-like qualities in His followers. We see by what Jesus said that genuine supportive friends do not give empty words and meaningless platitudes. The Apostle James helps us understand the power of Christ's words when he writes that, if our brother is without clothes or daily food and we tell him, "Go, I wish you all the best...be clothed and fed," we have just given empty platitudes. Jesus modeled supportive friendship by sending the Holy Spirit to His followers...not by giving empty platitudes about His coming departure from earth.

After Jesus finished giving His men their final marching orders, He went out to a garden called Gethsemane on the east side of Jerusalem. He told them to sit while He went to pray. Interestingly, He took Peter, James and John—His closest friends—with Him. He began to be sorrowful and troubled. Then He said to them, "My soul is overwhelmed with sorrow to the point of death. Stay here and keep watch with Me." Jesus was looking for support; He needed support. God made us to be social creatures, and we need the touch and support of others. A.T. Robertson, the great New Testament scholar, puts it this way, "The hour was late and the strain had been severe, but Jesus pleaded for a bit of human sympathy as He wrestled with His Father. It did not seem too much to ask. He had put His sorrow in strong language, 'even unto death', should have alarmed them." (Robertson, **Word Pictures in the New Testament**, 1930)

It is not a stretch to say that Jesus was looking for support from His friends in this time of agony and testing. Although they failed Him by falling asleep, the message is clear: if Jesus Christ the God/man, was depending not only on His Father God but also on His friends, then we, as men, must be willing to draw support from our friends, as well as give support to them.

We also learn from Jesus while He was hanging on the cross. He was hanging between two thieves who were also condemned to death and were in the process of dying. One of them was absolutely selfish and disrespectful, yelling at Jesus to get him off the cross if He were the Son of God. The second thief told the first thief to be quiet, acknowledging the divinity of Christ. Jesus, rewarding the second thief for his humility, promised him a place in heaven. The Bible is clear that when we genuinely worship God, we minister to Him. Obviously, in His perfection, He needs nothing from us. But He is desirous of our worship and adoration. It is not a stretch to say the repentant and humble thief on the cross worshiped Christ, the God/man, with his acknowledgement. In this acknowledgement, the second thief supported Christ's claim of who He was while on earth.

At one point while hanging on the cross, Jesus looked at His mother, acknowledged her, and said, "Behold your Son." Then to His best friend, John, whom He loved, He said, "Behold your mother." In other words, in the midst of the most hideous and most painful way to die at that time in history, we still see Jesus endeavoring to be supportive. He was not selfish. He wanted John to take care of His mother as if she were John's own mother.

Solomon helps us understand there are friends and then there are genuine friends. He says, "A friend loves at all times and a brother is born for adversity" and "A man of many friends comes to ruin but there is a friend that sticks closer than a brother." It is one thing to call someone friend; it is another thing to want only what is best for them, to be supportive of them, never to put them down and to consider how to "stimulate them to love and good deeds," as the author to Hebrew Christians writes.

Principles for Being a Supportive Friend

- True friends do not just enjoy one another; they also help one another grow.
- Being a supportive friend can take time, effort and energy.
- Being a supportive friend means we are there when our friend is in need or in trouble.
- It is good to evaluate ourselves to see if we are a true friend or only a friend of convenience.
- True friends are supportive friends.
- Friends of convenience like us when it is convenient for them.

Let's consider:

Supportive Friends	Friends of Convenience
Love us	Love self
Never compromise the truth	Always seek to please
Are useful for edification and growth	Are useless for edification and growth
Rebuke us	Do not rebuke us

If we are not careful, we can miss that when Christ was crucified to provide salvation for the world, He was also providing salvation for His friends. Consider the impact the crucifixion had on Peter, who denied Christ three times before the crucifixion, but after the resurrection was willing to be crucified for teaching the Good News as Jesus had instructed the disciples.

When we truly understand that we live under God's grace as a result of Christ giving His life for us, a fundamental and wonderful shift occurs in our Christian experience. Many Christians and church leaders communicate a guilt-inducing message that creates a fear of God that we can never measure up to His standards. BUT, when we genuinely understand Christ as our Savior and truly comprehend that through God's grace, our past, present and future sins are forever forgiven, and that the Holy Spirit is building Christ-like qualities in our lives, we become inspired to live our lives in a manner worthy of Christ.

We still fail both God and friends.

When we fail friends, sometimes they are not forgiving, which can be brutally painful, as it can be for them when the tables are turned. But we do not want to confuse imperfect human forgiveness with God's perfect forgiveness.

We don't have to fear not being forgiven by the perfect Forgiver. It is already done when we accept Christ. Nonetheless, as the perfect Forgiver, God knows it is best for us if we confess our sins—which means to agree with Him concerning our sins. Not because He doesn't already know, but because He wants us to acknowledge we know so we can grow in Christ.

For us, the wisdom and beauty of perfect forgiveness through perfect love is inspirational. The Bible tells us, "Perfect love casts out fear; fear is related to punishment. The person who fears does not understand God's love." We aspire to Christ-like lives not out of fear of punishment but out of gratitude for perfect love and forgiveness we don't deserve. As we grow into this Christ-like life, it is a far more fulfilling experience then our old life.

As we know, Christ-like friends are a special gift because within their support they understand our weaknesses, challenge us to grow and forgive us when we fail.

In the stories provided in this chapter, consider the amazing gestures of support provided for us (e.g., The Worst News Ever, Bailed Out in Boston, and More Support Than I Could Accept). Does support from friends of that magnitude create fear? Of course not. It inspires us to be better friends to those who support us as well as to other friends. It motivates us to live up to the quality of friendship we receive from our friends, just like a proper understanding of

God's grace inspires us to live our lives in a manner that shows genuine gratitude to Christ.

The principle is to exceed our friends' expectations when they need our support and to inspire them to be better as well.

The most basic and powerful way to connect to another person is to listen. Just listen.

Perhaps the most important thing we ever give each other is our attention.

A loving silence often has far more power to heal and to connect than the most well-intentioned words.
~ Rachel Naomi Remen

The holy passion of friendship is of so sweet and steady and loyal and enduring a nature that it will last through a whole lifetime, if not asked to lend money.
~ Mark Twain

It is difficult to say who does you the most mischief: enemies with the worst intentions or friends with the best.
~ Edward Bulwer-Lytton

More people are healed by friends listening to them than by counselors or pastors
~ Dr. Gary Collins

Discussion Questions and Applications

1. Can you describe a time when a friend was a "supportive friend" to you in a manner that far exceeded your expectations? What difference did it make in your life for the moment and for the future?

2. Do your friends perceive you as a supportive friend? Why?

3. The point has been made that genuine friends want the best for us and help us grow. How do you rank yourself in this area? Are you a genuine friend? How can you improve?

4. Supportive friends are friends of truthfulness. Why is this so?

5. How is being supportive an opportunity to share your faith?

6. If you were to list the top three friends you would call if you were in need of support, would you make the top three of their lists?

7. Are there stories you can share about support you have given or received that would be useful to your friends?

Chapter 6

Trust and Teach

There can be no friendship without confidence, and no confidence without integrity.

~ Samuel Johnson

Trust and Teach are two wonderful constructs that are corner-stones to high performance friendships. Trust pertains to having confidence in the integrity, strength and ability of a friend. Teach pertains to imparting knowledge or skill. When trust and teaching are combined, learning takes place. We are not speaking of the learning that occurs in the classroom, where it is safe, but rather that which takes place in our day-to-day lives—where we need to rely on friends and colleagues to teach us and allow us to teach them.

Jim was involved in investigating what allows a team of people to achieve high performance. Prior to conducting the research, such things as empowerment, resources, and skills were expected to be the elements that most contributed. Instead, they discovered that collaborative learning, the willingness of team members to teach and learn from each other, was the primary factor. When a team is organized, it is staffed with people with diverse skills to ensure that the collective expertise needed to get the task done exists. But the expertise has to be shared, taught and learned to have the most sustainable value.

The dynamic of teams in the workplace also applies to social set-tings. When two or more social friends gather for a purpose, whether it be recreational (e.g., golf or tennis); work related (e.g., a house project or moving); or a personal crisis (e.g., loss of a loved one or a child in trouble), both teaching and trust usually come into play. A person might benefit from a golf tip, but only if he is open to being coached. If someone has lost a loved one, a friend who has experienced a similar loss can be a gentle guide through the difficult process.

As we worked on this book, the reality of working together versus just being friends became readily apparent. As we collaborated, we learned a great deal about trusting each other, and therefore, we both grew and learned. Without the two-way trust and sharing of our different talents, the whole process could have easily been aborted when there were issues to resolve because the important ones required collaborative learning.

Yet comfort with both trust and teaching can be rare in relationships. And either can be easily lost if not treasured in a friendship. To ask someone to explain or teach something to us requires admitting our ignorance. We prefer to do that with someone we trust. We trust them to have the ability, but perhaps more importantly, we trust them to have the integrity to teach us in a helpful, non-critical manner. We want to feel safe when exposing ourselves to learning.

Let's explore how our friendships can become high performance when trusting and teaching are present.

Teaching and Learning from a Billionaire – Jim

I had the honor of serving on the Board of Directors of Best Buy for fourteen years as it grew from a five billion dollar company to a forty billion dollar company. The founder is billionaire Dick Schulze, an entrepreneur who is the real deal. He started with one store, mortgaged his home and experienced all you might suspect from those extraordinary people who add value to the world and create jobs. Dick never had a chance to go to college, but I learned more about business from him than from any business professor.

How could he enjoy such incredible success without a business degree? That question was answered early on as we were developing our friendship. One day in 1994, when the Internet was not as ubiquitous as it is today, I asked a question during a Board meeting—what was Best Buy doing about a company web page? Now keep in mind, web pages were quite new in 1994. Without hesitation or embarrassment, Dick looked me in the eye and said, "What's a web page?"

In that defining moment, I realized how an intelligent guy with a high school education could learn enough to become a multi-billionaire and create over 100,000 jobs. He wasn't afraid to ask a question and learn what he didn't know. It never crossed his brilliant mind to not do so.

The members of that Board have always been a special group, trusting each other enough to learn from each other. If you had been a fly on the wall in a board meeting, you would never have known that Dick was the founder and CEO. He is a man of great faith and humility. He never had a need to be puffed up nor assert his power over the rest of us. He knew that the best way to build and sustain a high performance organization was to draw from the collective strength of the team he had carefully put together.

Over the years, as our friendship grew, Dick and I had some intimate conversations about both professional and personal issues. I learned so much from what he taught me about business and life, I should have paid him tuition. But he gave me a full scholarship instead and some amazing stock options. I always felt that I could trust Dick to teach me and I was honored that he allowed it to be a two-way street.

Because of the tone set by Dick, the experience of being on the Best Buy Board was one of friends teaching and learning as a group. There were not only men on the Board; we also had some wonderful women leaders, adding to the quality of the experience. *Forbes* named Best Buy the best managed company in America. I believe that recognition came because of a Board where teaching and trust flourished.

A Friend Who Could Teach a Salesman and a Minister – John

I have a very dear friend, Doug, whom I met in campus ministry. He flew helicopters in Viet Nam, and he was in some rather tough situations, as you can well imagine. When he got home from the war, he went to a car dealer to buy a new car. He knew exactly what he wanted and the price he would pay. After he found the car he wanted and settled on the price he wanted, the salesman tried to persuade him to buy an entirely different car.

Doug grew exasperated and realized this salesman needed to be taken to school. He looked the man in the eye as he put his hand on the car and said, "I am going to buy this car, not the one you are trying to force on me. And I am going to buy it from a salesman I like. And, right now, I do not like you!"

As you can imagine, the shocked salesman had an amazing transformation as a result of a straight dose of honesty.

Even better is Doug's commitment to honesty with his friends. He has a desire to see them be the best they can be. Thus, he spares no punches. He is respectful, but he requires it in return. One time, he asked to see me for a talk. I thought he was going to ask me for some advice, but it turned out that I was the advisee—even though I was his boss. He looked me in the eye and said, "I have served under some very good leaders. You are the best. But you are also the most arrogant." Bam! A poke in the eye that I needed. I really did. And Doug's honesty started me on a process of looking deep into my soul to see why I was so wrong. Had Doug not made that honest commitment to our friendship, I would have needed to tell more humbling stories about myself in Chapter 2 on Humility!

My friend trusted that he could teach me an important lesson that I desperately needed to learn so that I could better myself.

118

You Pay What's Fair – Jim

I was horribly burned by a dishonest builder I contracted with to build a home I designed. He represented himself as a straight shooter and, for some time, I trusted him and believed we were becoming long-term friends. I was so angry when I learned much later that I had misread him. A good friend gave me a book about con artists. The book explained that con artists fool people because they are so good at it. The most common tactic is to falsely build trust on a few minor issues to set you up for the big ruse.

That was exactly what my builder did. Whenever there was a construction modification, our discussion and verbal agreement needed to be documented by a change order. Usually, there was no additional cost for the changes, and in one case, there should have been a huge savings. He would drag his feet on completing the change order documentation, but he always honored his word—at first. As construction got more complicated and more expensive, he fell further behind on documenting the verbal changes. I felt uncomfortable forcing the issue—I thought we were friends and there was no reason (yet) to be concerned. Towards the end of the project, I was presented with over $140,000 in additional bills for change orders I had been told would not impact the price. I couldn't believe it—and I couldn't see where there should have been any additional costs.

I thought I was protected by change-order language in the contract that said any changes to the construction project had to be documented and signed by me and the builder. But there is a regulation in construction law called quantum merit that says, even without change order documentation, if the builder can prove he incurred additional costs based upon claimed verbal agreements, a claim can be made for payment. If the payment claim is disputed, it can be settled in court.

Well, it took two years of litigation to sort this out. The builder could not prove he had incurred any additional costs. Instead, as I believed, he had in fact saved on the changes made. He even tried to claim his computer had damaged his cost accounting records when we pursued them through discovery. He dropped his claim the day before trial.

A few years later, I was going to build another custom home from a design on which I had been working. In the meantime, I had developed an extraordinary new friend, also named Jim, who was also a builder. As I talked to him, he taught me much about protecting myself better when building a house. So I explored the possibility of his building the new home for me and asked if he was interested and how his fees worked in a cost/plus contract.

To my amazement, he said, "Jim, I feel bad about what happened to you on your last house. (He was well aware of the nightmare I had been through with my previous builder.) Let's do this: I will oversee construction of your home as the general contractor; you pay all the bills directly to subcontractors and suppliers as we go, and that way there will be no overhead fees. When we are done, you can pay me what you think is fair."

That is what we did, and during the project, Jim taught me more about construction and how to be cost effective in constructing a home. He did an amazing job and completed the best construction I had ever experienced—no corners were cut. On top of that, he took care of warranty items and non-warranty items with integrity beyond that of any builder I had ever worked with before.

When we were all done, the hardest part was deciding on a fair fee for all of Jim's efforts. My greatest fear was to offer him less than he thought was fair. My economic (i.e., selfish) nature didn't want to stupidly pay too much (sorry about my dark side). Actually, I didn't figure Jim would allow me to pay too much, but I wanted to impress him that my proposed fee was legit and I also wanted to throw in a bonus.

I finally said Jim, "Please help me out. You have built a spectacular home. I really want to be fair, and most of all, I don't want to offer less than is fair even though I know you would take it and never complain. You are a friend of great value."

We finally agreed to arrive at our numbers independently and then reveal them to each other. Unbelievably, his number matched my estimate to the dollar—he had taught me well. I gladly paid him an extra 10% bonus and he remains a dear friend.

But Jim's friendship did much more. The previous builder had hurt me at two fundamental levels. First, he reduced my trust in people, and secondly, and more hurtfully, he reduced my trust in myself to assess whether someone was worthy of trust and friendship. Jim restored my faith in people and myself—a wonderful lesson.

A friend you can trust and learn from is invaluable.

To Grumble or Teach – John

I think of two men old enough to be my father. Both could have taught me. One did and became a friend; the other was a grump and I learned to ignore him.

I was a young man when I became a pastor. I knew there was plenty I did not know. There is still plenty I do not know. I still cringe at some of the mistakes I made in those early years, and I cringe at some of the mistakes I still make. But in spite of my humanity, the church grew and became a very exciting place in which to be involved.

People are always interested when they hear that, although I am a total abstainer, I do not think the Bible prohibits the drinking of alcohol. Drunkenness is a different matter, and I think that is wrong. I delivered a sermon on alcohol at our church, and later I saw a letter to the editor of our denominational magazine that subtly criticized my position. Then a newspaper featured an article where a number of us discussed the topic without attacking one another for our theological differences.

The reporter later told me she had received a call from a man in our church who had criticized our discussion and my position. It finally dawned on me. (Remember, I went to M.I.T. and sometimes it takes me a while.) This man, the grump, heard me speak every Sunday. But when he disagreed with me, he did not come to me. Rather, he triangulated—he told others, or, in the case above, he wrote a letter to the editor of a magazine. Apparently, he was not interested in helping me grow and learn; he was not interested in teaching me; he was interested only in being a grump.

Contrast this with Roy Jones. Our church desperately needed to add to the parking lot. We were given the money to buy the five acres behind and contiguous to our parking lot. Then a few neighbors fought the expansion—city hall meetings were not love-in meetings. The Minnesota Civil Liberties Union said they would defend us in court because our religious rights as a church were being denied. (My conservative friends have a hard time believing that, but it is true.) At any rate, my anger toward city hall spilled out in a sermon one day. It was totally inappropriate. A couple of days later a letter arrived from Roy Jones. In the letter, he told me how much he loved and respected me. He thanked me for my influence on his family. Then he corrected me for the anger I showed in the sermon. The letter ended with these words: "You are a better man than what we saw Sunday."

Because he cared, he reached out. He reached out in a respectful and affirming manner. He took a risk. His love was evident. His wanting the best for me was obvious. He helped me grow. We became friends. We are still friends.

What is the difference between the grump and Roy? One knew what he was against and knew how to complain in a way that did not edify anyone—especially me, who, in his mind, needed to grow. Roy knew what he was for, and he was honest in telling me. He told me in a way that affirmed me and in a way that I could receive. Roy was my teacher.

A friend said to me when he learned of the grump and Roy, "My best ever boss had two sayings: 1) 'not all learning experiences are positives'; and, 2) 'that fellow is not useless—he serves as a perfectly good example of how not to do things.' Your grump fits both of those. Whether interested in you personally or not, he did give you learning experiences. You saw the contrast—the helpful high road and the maligning low road. You saw the value of the high road and you took it."

Bullied by the NFL – John

I had finished the first draft of the above story, "To Grumble or Teach," and went to the gym to work out. I was working on a tough machine in a section of the gym that was vacant except for me. All of a sudden I heard a deep, gravelly, bossy voice behind me yelling, "Stand up straight...suck it in...you are compensating." I did not pay for a trainer, but I knew who it was without looking because I had often heard him in a room yelling at little kids. He was young enough to be my son.

So I stopped my exercise and stared at him. He then tried the power play on me and said, "I have a Masters degree in kinesiology, and I used to be a *recon* soldier in the military." I thanked him and then said, "It would have been polite to step around to face me when you yelled." He responded, "I used to work for the NFL and there is no polite in the NFL." As he walked away, I thought of those famous words from Jerry Glanville, the former coach of the Atlanta Falcons—"NFL...Not For Long"—somehow I thought they applied to this man.

I wondered, 'Should I use my trump card on him?' Tough decision—especially since this is a book about being Christ-like. I pondered...'What would Jesus do?' but had no inspiration. Then I thought, 'What would John do?' and I knew what I wanted to say. He came walking back by and I said, "Do you have a minute?" He said, "Sure." I said, "I have a different perspective on the NFL than you do." He answered gruffly, "Everyone has a perspective on the

NFL!" I said, "Well, mine comes from teaching Bible studies and speaking at chapel services for a number of NFL teams for a number of years and all the people with whom I worked (players, coaches, trainers and administrators) were always polite."

All of a sudden, that loud, gravelly, bossy voice was very quiet. I doubt he had ever had anyone call him on his NFL impolite shtick. He stuck out his hand and asked me my name. I shook his hand, told him my name and he walked away calling me "Sir."

If he had handled it the way Roy Jones had when I had expressed anger in the sermon, he would have stepped around, faced me and asked me if he could give me some advice. He might have attracted a new customer. But as it was, he violated a cardinal rule in the gym: you do not give unsolicited advice to a stranger or non-client unless he asks or he is risking injury.

A short time later, I bought him a book, **Quiet Strength: The Principles, Practices, and Priorities of a Winning Life** by former NFL Coach Tony Dungy, as a way to try to influence him. I had to leave the book at the front desk of the gym for him, so I included a note with it. About two weeks later I was leaving the gym as he was entering. I stuck out my hand, greeted him and called him by name. He said, "Good morning, sir." I reminded him my name is John. He said, "I know." When I asked him if he had gotten the book, he said, "Yes. Thank you very much. It is well read and well written." As we said goodbye, he said, "Have a good day, sir."

Who knows, maybe we will become friends.

In High Performance friendships, there is nothing like a friend you can trust and from whom you can learn.

Christ's Approach to Teaching and Trust

It is imperative we remember that Jesus was "full of grace and truth." His attitude, motivation and His words were all about helping people improve. His words were words of truth. No one ever had to wonder about the meaning of what He said. Truth is clear, understandable and honorable.

The Apostle Paul helps us understand how far reaching this quality of grace was that Jesus possessed; the quality He desires in His followers. The Apostle wrote, "Let your conversation be always full of grace, seasoned with salt, so that you may know how to answer everyone." Talking the way Jesus talked is being a servant; it is thinking of the other person and how he might receive words of challenge and teaching, then shaping our words so they are received and not just heard.

When Jesus taught His followers, "let your yes be yes and your no be no," He was telling us our words are to be sincere and clear. There can be no double-meaning or avoiding of issues. Jesus did not triangulate. He spoke what was on His mind to the one for whom it was intended and to the one whom it would challenge. When some Pharisees triangulated about Him at a dinner party, He did not duck the issue or the criticism. The Pharisees saw Him having dinner with some sinners and tax gatherers (think drug dealers in our society to understand the lack of respect people had for tax gatherers) and complained to some of His followers. He went straight to them and clarified that He came to help those who are spiritually sick.

By His response, we learn that triangulation is not an acceptable form of communication. In this interaction with the Pharisees, Jesus is living out Solomon's words, "Hear both sides of the story before you make up your mind." When we listen to a third party's description of a problem or teaching, his perspective is often colored or distorted. Jesus did not allow this to happen. He spoke directly to the Pharisees, saying what needed to be said. He did not have someone else say it for Him—and He did not say it to someone else.

Jesus said He "came to serve, not to be served." He was not talking specifically about teaching friends, but a principle can be drawn from His words. In His leadership, He was interested in preparing His men for continuing His message, and He was also interested in improving their character. He always had the intention of teaching and improving them, but His methods varied. He discerned the best method to get the message across. He seasoned His speech with grace, as with salt, so the listeners would be responsive.

Thus:

He taught Peter by 'poking him in the eye' and calling him 'Satan' when He told him to get behind Him because Peter was pushing his own agenda on Jesus.

He taught James and John by asking them if they were willing to die as He was going to die when they asked Him for the most prominent seats in heaven.

He taught Peter by telling him straight-out that Peter could not be His follower if he did not let Jesus wash his feet.

He was absolutely honest in teaching Peter about himself when Peter was bragging that he would die along with Jesus and Jesus told him he would deny Him three times before the rooster crowed in the early morning.

Jesus, as a servant/leader, was a teacher; He did not always lecture, but He was always teaching and changing His followers into better people. Even those who don't believe Christ is the Son of God acknowledge He was a great moral teacher as well as a great leader. He was always interested in the well-being of others. But it is an interesting question: if He were only a great moral teacher who falsely claimed to be the Son of God, how could He be genuinely moral? The fact is, great moral leaders do not lie. They speak "grace and truth."

Principles for Teaching and Trust

Genuine friends do not triangulate. Triangulation is gossip. It does no one any good: it soils the listener, it does not help the one who needs to hear and, by repetition, it reinforces a bad habit and practice on the part of the one doing it. Triangulation serves no positive purpose.

A counselor friend says, "Triangulation is a way to avoid intimacy; it allows one to be safe without being engaged with the person in order to help him. It is too bad too many tolerate it and think it is the way to handle difficult situations. The description that comes to mind is cowardly communication."

Genuine friends probably are not as honest about the warts in the lives of their friends as they are the warts in the lives of their spouses. We might see a friend once a month but we see our spouses every day, so we might be more tolerant in a friendship than we are with a spouse. But this kind of tolerance needs to be evaluated because it could well be that the friend's wart is a blind spot to him. Without a genuine friend raising the issue and teaching about it, the other friend might never learn and grow. Spouses work to make their marriages good and to improve each other. In this spirit, friends also need to raise issues.

Genuine friends are willing to risk being rejected, and they dare to raise issues in order to teach their friends. Taking these risks is not easy, but it is necessary.

Genuine friends endeavor to know their audience before they try to teach their friends. World Relief used to have a saying, "Empty bellies have no ears," meaning it is hard to tell someone about the Christian faith if they are starving. Genuine friends must have a similar attitude...what is the need of my friend when I share with him? How will my presentation make sense to my friend?

Genuine friends ask themselves if they are trustworthy. They might want to teach their friend for their own selfish reasons rather than for the friend's good and growth. Genuine friends want their friends to become better, so they are willing to teach them.

Anecdotal research we did underlines a couple of important principles:

- Men learn from men whom they respect
- Men learn from men who are consistent in their own lives
- Men do not listen to nor are they taught by friends who try to teach but do not show love and respect.

Thus, we need to make sure we are extending the invitation to our friends that we do want to learn from them. Additionally, we have to extend thanks and show receptivity when they do try to teach us

We cannot send mixed signals by asking for instruction and then become defensive when we get it. Conversely, we need to make sure our friends see consistency in our lives before we endeavor to teach them. Two parts to instruction are the offer and the receptivity. It is right to ask if we may offer instruction; it is wrong to offer instruction without making sure the receptivity is there.

One time on the golf course, John had a friend say, "May I tell you something?" John said, "No." When the man started to give instruction, John said, "You asked if you could offer advice. I said 'no' and so I do not want your advice at this moment." At the time, John was frustrated with his game and was not receptive to hearing any advice. Later, when he had calmed down, he was ready to listen.

There is a time to teach and a time not to teach. Trust is built when we learn to discern the difference.

Discussion Questions and Applications

1. Trust and truth are very important qualities in a genuine friendship. Why is it that we often do not trust our friends to have our best interests at heart when they step forward to teach us in order to help us improve?

2. How do we develop the self-effacing attitude that Dick Schulze manifested? Why do so many of us mistakenly think we need to advance ourselves or our agendas?

3. John's friend's poke in the eye was a poke of love. It made John a better man. Do we have men in our lives who love us enough to give us such a poke in the eye? Would we resist the poke or welcome it as a helpful gesture?

4. Complaining to someone else rather than the friend who needs teaching is non-productive and is triangulation. Why do we do it so often? How can we help our friends stop triangulating?

5. How can we prevent triangulation in our own communication? How do we help others avoid triangulating with us about others? Pointing to our ears and saying, "What do you think these are, garbage cans?" is probably not the way to do it. How can we do it?

6. Roy Jones manifested a lot of wisdom in his teaching letter that he sent John. What principles was he following in that letter?

7. In the story about NFL Impolite, can you think of a better way John could have handled the situation? How would you have handled it?

8. What stories about teaching and/or trust can you share in a helpful manner with your friends?

Chapter 7

Love and Loyalty

All love that has not friendship for its base is like a mansion built upon the sand.
~ *Ella Wheeler Wilcox*

Love is the only force capable of transforming an enemy into a friend.
Loyalty—In the end, we will remember not the words of our enemies, but the silence of our friends.
~ *Martin Luther King, Jr.*

Love and Loyalty are two of the greatest of human expressions and experiences. Love of a friend is a profoundly tender, passionate affection and warm personal attachment to another person. Loyalty to a friend involves faithfulness and devotion. Combined, these two constructs bring joy to a high performance friendship.

What would you say is easier for a man to do for a friend, demonstrate loyalty or express love? Have you noticed men are often not comfortable expressing love even to their wives? Have you noticed how rare it is for them to express it? There is a humorous but revealing story about the 80 year old couple, married 60 years, seeking marriage counseling. The counselor asks the wife, "What is the problem?" She responds, "He never tells me he loves me."

The counselor turns to the husband and asks, "Do you love your wife?"

"Sure," the husband responds.

"Then why don't you tell her?" asks the counselor.

The husband responds, "I told her I loved her 60 years ago when we first got married. Nothin's changed since then, so I didn't see any need."

We laugh about this but the truth is that it happens. John's grandmother wrote a poem about her husband—the family discovered it after she died. Her family did not know if she forgot about it, wanted it to be found or what she was thinking. However, it expresses great frustration and pain caused by a husband who thought only of himself. Obviously, if the man could not give himself to his wife, who was the proverbial saint, then he could not give himself to any male friend—something he never did to John's knowledge. Here's the poem:

My Husband

He never says, "I love you so,"
As I somehow thought he would,
But if I ask, he says, "You know I do;
That's understood."

He never says he likes my dress
Or likes the tune I'm playing,
But if I ask, he answers, "Yes,
That goes without my saying."

I ask him, "Will your love for me
Be always true and steady?"
He sighs and says, so wearily,
"I've told you that already."

"For better or worse," and more
The kind old parson chanted,
I don't know which I took Vern for,
But he took me for granted.

In the 1990's, there was a beer company that made hay with this reluctance of men to express love (you can still find the ads on *YouTube*). They made a series of commercials involving a man with tears in his eyes awkwardly expressing deep feelings to a friend. As the commercial concludes, you hear the man, with a lump in his throat and his overreaching words, "What I am trying to say is, I love ya, man!" His friend's expression changes from surprise to one of enlightened suspicion as he grabs his beer and says, "You can't have my Bud Light, dude." The humorous implication was that an emotional expression of love was really about getting his friend's beer.

In recent years, men have evolved from shaking friends' hands during greetings and farewells to a good hefty man-hug that usually involves two to three firm reciprocated pats on the back executed in unison. This is progress for men in expressing emotions.

We both confess to not telling friends we love them as we know we should. We both have lost loved ones and we know the regret of things left unsaid or undone, which has been poetically well expressed in this way:

The bitterest tear shed over graves are for words left unsaid and deeds left undone
~Harriet Beecher Stowe

We both are completely confident in our love and loyalty to each other. We demonstrate loyalty often but are less expressive about saying we love each other.

Bobby Knight or Brian Janz? – Jim

Brian Janz and I have a friendship where there is mutual love and loyalty. We met when he was a doctoral student at the University of Minnesota. He told me he had decided to get a PhD after his wife heard me speak at a seminar and told him, "I saw a guy doing what I think you would be happy doing. You need to go back to school."

Brian and I quickly became friends and enjoyed each other's commitment to humor as a way to get through life. Before Brian finished his PhD, I took a position as the FedEx Chaired Professor at the University of Memphis where I founded a research center funded by FedEx. The next year as Brian was wrapping up his degree, I desperately wanted to recruit him to Memphis because of his talent and, quite frankly, because working with him was a blast.

Fortunately, Brian felt the same way. With an opening available, it looked like smooth sailing. Unfortunately, the person negotiating the salary wanted Brian at Memphis less than I did—jealousy? So he made a low salary offer. I was not aware of the low-ball offer and didn't have an opportunity to remedy it before Brian accepted it out of loyalty. Brian later explained, "The opportunity for us to work together was more important than getting an offer that matched those that I received from other universities."

After we became colleagues instead of professor/student, our friendship grew stronger and we conducted research and published articles together that we are still proud of today. (Whenever I see Brian's name as a co-author on a manuscript, I have warm feelings.) Six years later, I was able to rectify his low salary in this rather unorthodox manner:

I had gotten caught in a bit of a political bind. The faculty revolted against the incumbent dean and she was removed. The president of the university asked me to step in as interim dean and to consider it as a permanent appointment. I was happy to help out because of the instability that existed, but I made it clear that I wasn't interested in the role permanently. In fact, I refused the additional compensation the president offered to avoid any appearance that I was opting for the position.

The president used an interesting strategy to encourage me to remain in this new role permanently—he made no effort to recruit a new dean. I was stuck for over a year in a job I didn't want that was taking a toll on my research, authoring and speaking tours. Have you ever seen the movie Ground Hog Day starring Bill Murray? The premise is that Bill Murray's character is stuck living the same day over and over no matter what he does. I felt the same way. Every morning, I would wake up and I was still the dean, in spite of my wishes to be otherwise.

In the midst of this never-ending saga, my alma mater, Texas Tech, called and asked if they could entice me to return to Tech by offering an endowed chair. Their timing couldn't have been better—an escape plan!

The problem: How could I abandon Brian, a loyal friend with whom I loved to work? The solution: Take Brian with me. I told Texas Tech it was a package deal. This was a win/win because we could now get Brian's salary up to where it should have been and Tech would get a rising star in Brian. But Memphis knew what they had in Brian and they just countered and increased every offer I could get Texas Tech to make—something Memphis had been unwilling to do until they were at risk of losing him.

In a last effort, after singing the praises of Brian, I made a personal appeal to the president of Texas Tech to match the latest offer from Memphis. The president looked at me calmly and said, "Jim, we are trying to negotiate with Bobby Knight to be our basketball coach, and we only have so much money to go around. You are an alum of Texas Tech, so let me ask you, "Who do you think will do more to add to the prestige of Texas Tech, Bobby Knight or this Bobby Janz?"

I said, "But his name is Brian."

The president said, "My point exactly."

At that point I knew my situation was hopeless!

The bad news: I didn't get Texas Tech to match Brian's Memphis offer. The good news: Memphis increased Brian's salary by 80% and Brian not only understood but also encouraged my career move. More importantly, love and loyalty had been expressed both ways. Brian remains a close friend to this day, even though we no longer work together directly. We still share personal conversations where the advice and guidance of a friend is most treasured. Recently, we caught up with each other at a conference and sat at the same table from lunch until the restaurant closed at midnight. My wife and her best girlfriend would have been jealous of the intimacy of that conversation.

Friend, We Can Do Great Things Together – John

Someone once said that when you are a college or seminary president you get to live in a big house, drive a big car, walk to work...and beg for money. From my perspective as a former seminary president, the fund-raising part is a reality—it is part of the job. There is another part that many people do not consider: the number of people who want to be friends and have great aspirations for what they and you, as president, can do together. Sometimes it is hard to discern their sincerity.

One such man, "Jack," was the pastor of a large church and shortly after my arrival as president he began to tell me how thankful he was that I was in town. In my ignorance, I thought it was the beginning of a good friendship. When I abruptly resigned for reasons that do not need to be discussed in this book, I endeavored to meet with every donor and pastor I had befriended on behalf of the seminary before I left town.

I had a meeting with Jack and another pastor, and when I arrived, the other pastor told me Jack said I was out of the will of God for resigning my position. When Jack arrived, I asked him directly if he thought I was out of the will of God for resigning. He answered, "That would not be my decision to make." I looked at the other pastor, who just shrugged his shoulders. I think we both realized Jack was loyal only to himself. I was sorry for Jack and decided I had been fooled.

That lack of loyalty and lack of truthfulness opened my eyes to what often happens. Later, I was flying on a ministry trip, and the president of a national Christian organization sat down beside me.

I think I had met him only two or three times before. He began to tell me confidentially about people in his organization.

For a while, I was thinking, 'I must be very smart and wise because he wants a relationship with me and he wants my advice.' When I began to advise him, however, it was obvious he was not interested in my advice. Rather, he was gossiping about people in his organization, and I was amazed at his lack of loyalty to his employees and fellow ministers. I began to wonder, 'If he talks about his colleagues to me, I wonder what he would say about me to his colleagues?' Later in the rental car as I was driving to my speaking assignment, I realized he had been disloyal to his people and had gossiped about them to a man he hardly knew.

Often, people talk to me about some of their best friends! They have told me about their friends being overweight or preaching too long, and have complained about their own and their friends' wives marital problems. Accepting the fact that I am not so smart and that often people do not want a relationship with me nor do they want my advice, I try to stop such talk by changing the subject or saying, in a most subtle way, "If you talk to me this way about 'Bob,' how do you talk about me to Bob?" It might not be very polite, but it is better than letting someone gossip about his good friend.

This issue of disloyalty or lack of loyalty to friends is compounded by the use of Twitter and email. The lack of loyalty is often couched in words such as, "We need to pray for that man." Indeed, when I resigned from the seminary, I heard that a man who I thought was a friend had said to someone, "We need to pray for Vawter." But he never called to ask why I resigned or if I was doing okay—which in fact I was. I realized he was not a loyal friend; it appeared he was loyal only to himself—which is selfishness.

Contrast this to a long-time friend with whom I have walked through some deep waters. When he called to tell me he was in some trouble that could affect him financially and work-wise, I called him a very strong name (which cannot be repeated here). He was taken aback and thought I was mad at him for the situation in which he found himself. Actually, I was upset with him because the situation had been brewing for years, and he had never confided in me. I never knew about it until he called to tell me he was in trouble. I do not know if I could have helped him but I could have walked the lonely and painful road with him. He had been walking that awful path for years and he had been walking it alone. No one should have to walk such a path alone. If he were in trouble, I wanted to be walking with him. That is what friends do.

Later, he was in a situation where a person began talking to him about what a jerk I am. (I wonder how the person figured it out, since I thought I had done a good job hiding it.) He told me he stopped the conversation cold by saying, "I have been friends with John for a long time and you are not describing the man I know." He said the person did not know what to say and grew quiet. My friend was loyal to me—more than he was to himself because he risked rejection and wrath to tell my critic that what was being said was untrue.

My friend helped me learn that friends are loyal. Friends do not talk to others about you in a negative way. And friends do not allow others to talk to them in a negative way about their friends when the friends are not present. Sadly, I have lost count of the number of times that people have gossiped to me about even their best friends. I am sorry I let it happen. I still regret my reluctance to speak up as I should have done. As I said above, I used to think I was real smart and trustworthy. Now I realize it was just a convenient opportunity for them to gossip and malign their friends—sad but true.

Recently, Susan and I were visiting friends in another town—a small town. I went to the local gym to work out, and as I was lifting weights, two men began talking about Bill. I had no idea who Bill was, but I heard that "he had a temper on the golf course, was not honest, does not compete hard when they play tennis and they do not like him." It was such a despicable conversation that at one point I was tempted to ask, "Which Bill are you talking about?" When they answered, I was going to say, "Oh, yes, he is my brother," just to see what they would do. I know it would have been a lie, but it would have been interesting to watch their reactions. Thankfully, I was able to shove that dark side of me back inside and keep my mouth shut. Again, this talking about friends when they are not present is sad but true…very sad.

Friend or Work Wife? – Jim

My wife, Brynn, amazes me. She is brains and brawn. She is a two-time national champion, all natural, (i.e., no steroids) body builder who has prevailed over women less than half her age. She is only 5' 1" tall, and when she competes, she weighs 100 lbs. She has bench pressed my weight of 210 lbs and is also smart and wise. Her counsel is so helpful in so many ways. We are open and trusting in our communication. She is my best friend.

Though she is intelligent and well read, she doesn't have all the experiences I have from academia. She can provide useful perspective and insight from a different point of view but cannot draw from the specific expertise of a faculty colleague.

That is where Jim Hoffman comes in. I had returned to Texas Tech to give back to my alma mater. I met Jim at a faculty meeting where he introduced himself and said he had worked with one of my former Memphis doctoral students at Florida State. Jim explained he couldn't believe all the skills the young man had for interacting with corporations to conduct research, so he asked him where he had learned all this, and the man answered, "Jim Wetherbe."

Jim went on to explain how pleased he was that I had returned to Tech and hoped we could work together, as he wished to learn from me. Actually, Jim was already full of great ideas for Texas Tech, including building a physician's MBA program, a JD MBA program and an executive-style MBA. With an executive MBA, we could attract students—primarily *alums*—from Dallas, Houston, San

Antonio, etc., back to the Rawls College of Business at Texas Tech, using a weekend and internet-based distance learning program.

As the conversation progressed, Jim asked if I could provide seed money to start these programs. He wanted only $1,800, which I figured was a small risk for someone who might or might not be complimenting me on my career with sincerity. It turned out to be my best Return on Investment (ROI) in academia.

He got the money and then amazed the entire university. Jim was a solid researcher and, additionally, had entrepreneurial skill and drive. Within a couple of years, we had three hundred new MBA students who, because of the quality of the program, were great promoters of the MBA program Jim had designed. The programs were generating millions of dollars with healthy margins for the university at a time when budgets were being cut by the state. We became the largest graduate program on campus.

Though Jim deserved the credit, he would always tell me how grateful he was to have me for a mentor. I have tried to convince him for years that it is a quid pro quo relationship. I started learning as much or more from him years earlier. But he is humble and resists the accolades.

Jim and I can have as many as five phone conversations in a day that on occasion last up to an hour. Though we focus on work issues, we readily fall into personal discussions about family and other personal issues, including faith. We often compare notes on child rearing and marital insights.

Because of the time Jim and I spend in personal and work conversation, my wife has affectionately tagged him my work wife. Funny at first—Jim and I now consider it a compliment.

Our wives obviously come first, but Jim and I have an extraordinary friendship based upon love and loyalty. Jim once said, "You are one person I know who would never cut my legs out from under me at work or otherwise." He knows I feel the same about him.

Loyalty Can Precede Friendship – John

When I was pastoring in Minnesota, a group in the church wanted it to take a different direction than the pastors or board believed it should take. The group wanted the church to get involved in their political agenda rather than teach Jesus' good news and help people deepen their Christian faith.

This kind of pressure was not unique to our church. It happens all the time; it is simply part of the privilege and pain of leadership. It cannot be avoided. As often happens and will continue to happen, some of the criticisms were not very kind or edifying and they were directed at the primary leader—me. The criticisms did not feel good, but I believed we were on the right path and I was not going to be dissuaded from that path.

One day I saw on my calendar that a man in the church—one I hardly knew beyond a brief greeting on Sunday mornings—had set up a lunch appointment. I had no idea why we were meeting. I assumed it was for more than the meal. And I was right. Gary told me during lunch that I was doing a wonderful job, that he knew I was being criticized (I did not know he was friends with one of the main criticizers) and that I should keep the church headed down the path we had taken. That was the start of a great friendship that continues today.

Gary moved to Arizona before Susan and I did. When I became president of Phoenix Seminary, I asked him to be on the board and he accepted. His loyalty to me was obvious. But his loyalty to Christ and his loyalty to the seminary were stronger. Thus, when he thought my thinking was incomplete or needed refining in some presentation I was making to the board, he was quick to say what he thought. His loyalty to the friendship meant he could not compromise the truth or his perspective on the issues the board discussed.

Compare this with a board member of another Christian institution who bragged that he would lie for his president because of their friendship. Is that loyalty? Loyalty means we want the best for our friends. But lying or withholding truth do not help someone become a better person. Rather, such lack of truth stymies the growth in that person's life.

As the friendship has grown, Gary and I have been involved in ministry together and done international ministry trips together. The issues of trust and loyalty go hand in hand. Both of us have feet of clay up to our eyeballs and can be caustic. Thus, we often ask each other to be the sounding board when we think our attitudes about or responses to a situation might be less than Christ-like. We can trust the loyalty of one another because we both understand our first loyalty is to Christ and how He wants us to live our lives. Knowing that a friend is more loyal to Christ than he is to you makes him a great friend. His loyalty to Christ means he cannot lie or compromise on the truth when you are asking him to be your sounding board. He has to look you straight in the eye and tell you that you are on or off base.

Years ago when I was David Harowitz's pastor, he was on the board of the church. David is the Jewish attorney whom I love and respect so much. Quite frankly, there was a man, "Tom," who was not qualified to be on the board, did not make any contributions of wisdom to the board, was negative in everything he said and would have been fired from the board had he not resigned before we could fire him. How he got on the board, I do not know. One day, Tom said some unkind things about other board members and me, and then left. I watched David's response and I knew by his non-verbal communication that he did not agree with Tom.

The next morning, I sent him this email message: "David, this note is about genuine friendship. After the meeting was over, I felt sad about and for Tom because of his behavior. This note is not about Tom. I was thinking about my friendship with you and the confidence I have in that friendship, and I thought, if David thought I had issues where I was/am wrong, he would tell me because he wants me to be better and grow. He knows I love Christ and that I want to be conformed to the image of Christ. I can be confident in that and that allows me to move ahead. On the other hand when there is no genuine friendship, the person just moves away from you and makes little or no effort to help you grow. You cannot be confident in that. Nor do you want to be around those kinds of people. So, I just want to thank you for being a true and genuine friend. It started with the mean Jewish lawyer correction and has grown from there. Thanks, friend, for being a good friend."

Loyalty and trust are absolute prerequisites for achieving high performance friendships.

Christ's Approach to Love and Loyalty

Jesus was always profound and to the point. He was even more so when He pulled His disciples into the Upper Room in Jerusalem to give His final marching orders to His men before He went out to be crucified. Every word counted at that point. Jesus was economical in His words. Thus, we need to pay close attention, especially when He says, "Everyone will know you are My disciples if you love each other." Jesus is so clear—love is key.

John has spent a lot of time in the seminary listening to people argue the finer points of theology beyond what is healthy. Often, those arguments/discussions seemed like a wrestling match without love. But Jesus says love is key. We recognize that much of our culture is opposed to Christ's teaching. Men treat each other like bears in the forest, swatting each other rather than saying, "I love you." So Christ challenges us as men to come up to His standards rather than lowering ourselves to our culture's standards.

Jesus defines this love when He says we are to love our neighbor as ourselves. Jesus was absolutely introducing a new concept into the society in which He lived because it was not a loving culture and love was not easily expressed. When Jesus was telling the people to love their neighbors as they loved themselves, someone asked who his neighbor was. Jesus answered by telling a parable about a man who was robbed, beaten and left in a ditch. Everyone walked by him except the outcast—the man from Samaria. The Samaritan took care of him, paid his lodging at an inn and fed him. The truth is clear—if we are to love and reach out to the man in the ditch whom we do not know, how much more should we reach out and express love to our friends?

Neibuhr talks about Christ being above culture. We try to bring Him down to our culture, but He is above culture. Thus, He sets the standards for how we live and love. Life is a process of becoming conformed to His image. Christ extends grace and forgiveness to us, and our response to that grace and forgiveness should be to become more like Him—and love as He explained.

The Fruit of the Spirit is the explanation of the qualities Christ wants to build in our lives. Faithfulness is one of those qualities. In being faithful, we are emulating Christ's faithfulness and loyalty to us. When John's friend refused to allow him to be criticized when he was not present, he was being Christ-like in his loyalty and faithfulness to the friendship with John. Jesus defended His followers to the Pharisees, who criticized them for breaking the dietary law of washing their hands before they ate. Jesus did not capitulate: He did not bow to peer pressure. He spoke truth in explaining why they did what they did.

Solomon helps us understand the value of genuine friendship when he writes that there are some who call us friends but they will not carry any load for us. He contrasts this to the one who sticks closer than a brother. He also says many make claims of being a friend but a faithful friend is not an easy find. Again, we see this faithfulness manifested in the life of Christ—how He remained faithful and loyal to His friends in spite of pressure from the Pharisees.

Solomon also helps us understand that genuine friends do not always agree with us. Genuine friends correct, teach and confront us. He says that hidden love is not as valuable as open rebuke.

Thus, we need to be corrected. The friend who does not tell us the truth does not help us grow. Solomon uses the analogy of two pieces of iron rubbing together until they are smooth to describe how one sharpens his friend. And He tells us that wounds from a friend can be trusted but the kisses of an enemy are bitter.

Love for and loyalty to a friend do not mean we are willing to compromise truth or ethics for the sake of that friend. The Bible is clear that there is no partiality with God. He does not bend the truth for His favorites. We see this in Christ's rebuking of Peter. Even though Peter was one of His closest friends, Jesus corrected him firmly when Peter needed it. And we certainly see it in Christ crying out to the Father as He hung on the cross, "My God, My God, why have You forsaken Me?" Christ had taken the sin of the world and our sin into His body, so the holy God had to turn His back on His Son. God the Father was not partial. Sin separates us from God. Christ had become sin and was separated from God the Father on our behalf. Genuine friends do not pull their punches when their friends need to be punched. Genuine friends help each other grow.

Finally, Jesus teaches us something about the loyalty and love of friendship in Peter's denial of Him. Who of us can say we would not have made the same betrayal that Peter made. We should not criticize him because we have not been in his shoes; we do not know the pressure and fear he felt at the moment. It is amazing how Christ predicted the denial and yet remained loyal to Peter. Peter failed Jesus but Jesus did not fail Peter. And this gave Peter courage, and he rose to the loyalty of a true friend when he was crucified for preaching the good news as instructed by his friend Jesus. Love and loyalty allow forgiveness for weakness. That love and loyalty inspire loyalty for the future. The Apostle Paul challenges us to be loyal and forgive, just as Jesus did, when he writes that we are to forgive each other—just as in Christ, God forgave us.

Principles of Love and Loyalty

Socrates once asked a simple old man what he was most thankful for. The man replied, "That being such as I am, I have the friends that I have had."

A friend is one who knows you and still loves you. Genuine friends reveal themselves to each other. And genuine friends know each other, warts and all.

"What have I done with my life that someone would call me his best friend?" is a question that can easily be a life principle that motivates genuine friendship. Giving love and loyalty to friends is one of the prerequisites for such friendship.

"It is better to give than to receive." Genuine friends are not always giving; they are also on the receiving end, so allow someone to enjoy the privilege of giving.

Being friendly with someone is not the same as being friends. Friends are intimate with and loyal to one another.

A friend is one who knows you as you are, understands where you have been, accepts who you have become and still gently invites you to grow.

Genuine friends tell the truth—not just what someone wants to hear. Genuine friends have a way of staying close and poking one another in the eye when needed. Genuine friends know the pitfalls of the future and warn each other about them.

Genuine friends do not show partiality. Impartiality helps us understand that our friends really do love us. Donovan Campbell says of his time as a Marine in the Middle East, "To my surprise...I found out my Marines would accept even the harshest punishment with equanimity provided that...they were confident that the punishment's administrator would have doled out the same punishment to anyone else in the situation" (Campbell, **Joker One**, 2009).

146

Discussion Questions and Applications

1. Why is it that we tend to try to bring Christ down to our cultural level rather than seeing Him as above culture?

2. Jesus was loyal to His friends when the Pharisees were critical of them. This quality of loyalty is not always a quality we see today. Explain why.

3. Jesus was clear in explaining the importance of being loving people. Yet men have a hard time expressing love to men. Why do we struggle with this expression that was so important to Christ?

4. John's grandmother wrote a heart-breaking poem about her husband. Do you agree that if a man cannot express love to his wife, and if he is going to be selfish with her, he will not be able to express love to his male friends, if he has any?

5. Why is it that men often feel the need and the freedom to talk about others when they are not present? What does this do to the listener? What does it do to the one doing the speaking?

6. How do we as friends make sure we are not compromising the truth or being partial when we see that our friends need to be told about a blind spot they have?

7. How can we as men help one another grow in the areas of love and loyalty with our friends?

8. What stories of love and loyalty can you share in a manner that would be helpful to your friends?

Chapter 8

Independence and Inner Compass

If one is estranged from oneself, then one is estranged from others too. If one is out of touch with oneself, then one cannot touch others.
~ Anne Morrow Lindbergh

Friendship with oneself is all important because without it one cannot be friends with anybody else in the world.
~ Eleanor Roosevelt

Independence pertains to freedom from the control and influence of others. *Inner* pertains to the mind or spirit, and a *Compass* is a reliable reference for determining directions. High performance friendships can encourage us in both our independence and keeping our inner compass regulated to a true north.

C. S. Lewis, a distinguished professor in England, describes how he was transformed from an atheist to a Christian in his book **Mere Christianity** (Harper, 1952, renewed, 1980). The foundation for this transformation is expressed in his compelling observation:

These, then, are the two points I wanted to make. First, that human beings, all over the earth, have this curious idea that they ought to behave in a certain way, and cannot really get rid of it. Secondly, that they do not in fact behave in that way. They know the Law of Nature: they break it. These two facts are the foundation of all clear thinking about ourselves and the universe we live in.

That was written over 50 years ago, but to illustrate the universality of his observation, consider the following Cherokee Indian parable: An old Cherokee Indian was telling his grandson about a fight that goes on inside him. He said the fight is between two wolves: One wolf is evil: anger, envy, sorrow, regret, greed, arrogance, self-pity, guilt, resentment, inferiority, lies, false pride, superiority and ego. The other wolf is good: joy, peace, love, hope, serenity, humility, kindness, benevolence, empathy, generosity, truth, compassion and faith.

The grandson thought about it for a minute and then asked his grandfather, "Which wolf wins?"

The old Cherokee simply replied, "The one I feed."

We all live by some particular set of standards. Even those who say they are independent thinkers and want no standards have an internalized set of standards—themselves and their own thinking. These personal standards for life are our "inner compass." Just as the traveler needs his literal compass to navigate the surface of the earth or the ocean, each of us needs some kind of inner compass to navigate the twisting paths of life and friendship. This inner compass dictates how we think and live, and helps us know if we are on the track toward deeper friendships. We all want to be independent, but the fact is we are dependent on our inner compass. And it is imperative that our compass be true and not erratic, bending to whatever we want to do regardless of the morality of the action or impact on other people.

A person's standards might not be carefully thought out, well-defined or altruistic in nature, and they might not even be aligned with any specific truth. They might be humanitarian and kind, or they might be patently self-serving and self-centered. They might be based on nothing more than the selfish pursuit of pleasure or material goods. A person's standards might be centered on God and the Bible as the never-changing north setting on their inner compass—or they might reject His ultimate truth. Even those who lack any sort of moral values or ethical standards—those whose lives are built around self-gratification or the accumulation of wealth—organize their lives around some set of standards or principles. Sadly, too many people build their standards and values on foundations that are, at best, faulty.

A common question raised by people of faith is, "What about those who don't have access to religious teachings such as the Bible?" If we take the quotes above and add to them what Paul says in Romans, we get the answer:

For since the creation of the world, God's invisible qualities—His eternal power and divine nature—have been clearly seen, being understood from what has been made, so that men are without excuse.

If we believe in God, we can reasonably conclude we all have a God consciousness within us. We either respond to it or we reject it regardless of our access to formal religious resources. God promises that if we respond to this consciousness and seek Him, we will find Him. Specifically, we are told in Jeremiah, "You will seek Me and find Me when you seek Me with all your heart." In Jim's book, **Faith Logic**, he acknowledges that the results of his seeking were greatly enhanced when he added the "all your heart" part.

One of the beautiful truths about God is that He never forces Himself on us—He lets us choose to accept or reject Him.

We believe upon our seeking and finding, God reveals Himself to us in manners that enhance our inherent inner compass—our sense of right and wrong. We can also attempt to ignore that inner compass and, over time, render it less relevant as a guide to how we choose to live.

As a professor of Information Technology, Jim likes to use the Internet as a metaphor to help understand the connection to God (**Faith Logic**). If we choose, we can go online with billions of people and wirelessly access a wealth of information and software applications on the Internet. Much of what we access can be downloaded and become part of our computer systems. Similarly, we have wireless access to God—to His infinite wisdom and guidance which can be downloaded and become part of who we are and how we live our lives. We also have to be mindful of enemy software (e.g., viruses and worms) that try to destroy our systems and information.

Our inner compass serves to guide us, but we are even better served by also seeking God's wisdom and guidance. All of us must remain independent from influences that mislead us in destructive directions (e.g., pornography, and deceptive and risky social networking).

Let's explore the dynamics of independence and our inner compass with a few stories and then see how, through Christ, we can reduce our self-inflicted hardships brought on by bad decisions.

Accounting Fraud – Jim

It is heartbreaking to see people make decisions that, at least in this life, are unfixable, e.g., Bernie Madoff's financial fraud that destroyed thousands of people's retirement funds; the Enron management and board fraud scandal; or even former President Nixon's Watergate scandal that forced a brilliant leader to resign in shame. A Texas Tech alumnus named Benny Judah was a rising star entrepreneur with a small diversified investment empire. He over-extended with day-trading stock losses and started covering them with money from other investors. It all collapsed—he lost everything and was sentenced to jail.

These tragic stories start with less consequential distortions of the inner compass. Success with deceit leads to greater temptation and greater risk. When a criminal is caught, it is troubling to hear people say, "That was dumb." Is it not more significant that it was wrong? Implied in the former statement is that smart and wrong (i.e., he got away with it) is acceptable. Dumb and wrong is just… well…dumb.

I did something as a student years ago that I kept secret until recently. As an undergraduate, I was taking an accounting class that I found boring. The professor, an elderly man, talked in a perfect monotone and read his notes. If he detected someone was not listening, he would continue lecturing, develop a question and then, at the surprise of the distracted student, loudly call his or her name. He seemed to relish when a student didn't even know the question let alone the answer.

A few weeks into the semester, he started missing classes regularly—he just didn't show up. We knew the rule was that students were to wait ten minutes, and if the professor didn't arrive, class was canceled. We started hoping he wouldn't show and he did not disappoint us. We learned later that he was an alcoholic and that was the cause of his irresponsible behavior.

To my inner compass, not having class seemed wrong, but I, along with the other students, justified that it was not our fault. As time passed we as a class realized we had to take a standardized accounting test to get credit for the course. So we went as a group to alert the Dean of the Business School to the problem. To our horror, he replaced the professor with the professor we had all avoided like the plague by taking this class—the dreaded Professor Haight (pronounced HATE)—enough said.

As the standardized test date approached, Professor Haight's lectures confirmed how little we had learned. In the midst of our despair, a student in the class informed us he had access to a fraternity test file with the standardized accounting test answers. We rejoiced; copies were made and given to all members of the class.

No mistake—this was cheating, but we all rationalized that we had no choice. My inner compass challenged me but it didn't stand a chance. I logged off from my online connection to God and did what I needed to do. We all passed, never got caught and moved on.

I can't say there was peer pressure among us—it was more peer anxiety and jubilant collaboration.

I buried what I had done for years. As I became a young professional, I did something worse—I would retell what happened as a humorous story. I would tell of the tension in the room as we all waited to see if the actual test was the same as the fraternity test—if not, we were out of luck. We had just memorized answers with no true understanding of accounting. I could tell as I sat in the back of the room when one by one the body language revealed that we were safe.

I've made my share of mistakes in life when I have not taken direction from my inner compass and made prayerfully considered decisions benefitting from the love and wisdom of God.

Recently, I was asked, as an alumnus of Texas Tech, to give the welcome address to each incoming class of MBA students. After the Bernie Madoff incident became big national news and the Bennie Judah story made local news, I decided to tell an additional message to these young men and women. I confessed to cheating on my accounting test. I tell them I never suffered the type of consequences of Bernie or Bennie but I suffered nonetheless. I could have been expelled from school and had my academic record blemished forever. As a Professor of Business, my punishment is living with the stain of having cheated on a test as a student. I tell the incoming students that though it is something I did decades ago, it still haunts me today as a better and wiser man. I caution them that small acts of deceit can lead to bigger acts. It embarrasses me to tell that story but it strengthens my independence and inner compass to do so.

Values versus Absolute Truth – John

Jim's story above was news to me. I did not know the story until I read it in the draft he sent to me. His feeling of guilt raises a very interesting point pertaining to the question: is it accounting fraud or academic opportunity? And, as I tell a similar story, we must make sure we discern the difference between our values and the absolute truth of Jesus as our inner compass. Also, if I had known Jim was going to make his confession, I would have congratulated him, smiled and then said, "Remember, Jim, confession is good for the soul but bad for the reputation."

I, too, benefitted from the use of fraternity test files. I think of one five-hour class where I received an A because I had the benefit of the tests the professor had used in the past. I did not see it as cheating; I saw it as an opportunity. When he returned the tests to us, he did not say or write on the tests, "Not to be shared with any-one else." So from my point of view it became public property and was open to being shared with others. All these years later, I still do not believe it is cheating. If a professor is too lazy to outthink and outwork the students, he or she should not be a professor.

Jim and I had a great discussion about our different responses to what we did. It is very important to note we were discussing our values and not absolutes. Jim made a strong case for it being unfair for a student to have such an advantage. I completely understand and respect his position. I believe this underlines the evidence of a great friendship—healthy discussion over a dis-agreement of values without badgering, criticizing or diminishing each other.

This difference of perspectives between us leads to the very inter-esting point of the difference between our values and absolute truth. A church, suffering from the impact of a great sexual indiscre-tion on the part of their pastor, invited me to speak to their mem-bers. The scandal had hit the front page of the newspapers and the television news in that area. The pastor had to resign in dis-grace. There was a lot of tension and sadness when I arrived to speak four times that weekend—to try to calm the waters and make some sense out of what had happened. I believe God used me to help the church members see that tomorrow could be a better day and that God was not finished with them as a church.

Seven weeks later, I was called back to speak because the former pastor was starting a new church seven miles away from where he had previously been for many years. As I pondered in Arizona what

I would say before I flew to that city to speak, I really agonized. As a guest speaker (and healer), I could not avoid the issue. It had to be hit head on—I could not be subtle. Many of the four thousand people in the church were confused, angry, disillusioned and skeptical over the former pastor's decision to start another church so close to them. People needed answers and the answers needed to be clearly stated and easily understood.

It was at this point that I settled on the belief that there is a difference between a value and an absolute truth. For example, I have a value that I should not drink alcohol. It is not an absolute truth; it is just my value. I would be wrong if I tried to project my value on other people. On the other hand, I believe there is an absolute truth that stealing is wrong, so if a friend of mine were stealing, I would speak up.

I had two points in mind as I spoke to the issue of the former pastor starting a new church. One point was to look at our own sin and inconsistencies through two of Christ's warnings: that we should take the "log out of our own eye before we take the speck of dust out of our brother's eye"; and, "You who are without sin cast the first stone," when He spoke to the crowd that was angry over the woman caught in adultery. My second point was that my values would not allow me to start a new church seven miles away but there is no absolute truth in the Bible that forbids it. I asked people to consider the difference between our values and God's absolute truth, and not to project their values on their former pastor.

Parenthetically, one of my best friends did something similar a few months later. He resigned from one church over a matter of conscience and a disagreement with the board, and organized a group into a church just a few miles away. When he asked my opinion on what he was doing, I told him my values would not allow me to do it, and I wished he would not, but I did not think there was any absolute truth in the Bible that precluded him from doing it. I also told him that because my values were against his doing it, I could not give him advice on what he was doing. To his credit, he understood my values and never asked for my advice. We were able to have the same spirit in our discussion and disagreement that I mentioned above relative to the disagreement that Jim and I had over the use of test files.

Finally, let's go back to my M.I.T. days. Once, on my way to take a Sociology mid-term exam, a fellow student I knew quite well offered me the test answers. He had arranged for a friend of his to dress as a custodian and go to the faculty area and steal the test. In this case, I refused the help. Absolute truth against stealing would not allow me to do it.

When You're Clearly Outvoted – Jim

Serving on Boards of Directors is an exciting way to learn and make a difference. It is not without its problems, and one takes on considerable financial and reputational risk to be a board member due to shareholder and regulatory accountability.

For the most part, board experiences have been rewarding for the ten or so boards on which I have served over the years. I am humbled by the generous nature of entrepreneurs I have had the opportunity to work with, such as Dick Schulze of Best Buy, Fred Smith of FedEx and Bob Stevenson of CIBER. They are all over-achieving risk takers who create jobs for hundreds of thousands of people. Their philanthropic gestures involving millions of dollars are stellar, as is their integrity.

Here is a revealing anecdote. When I was still a Professor at the University of Minnesota and serving on the board of Best Buy, the development group at the University invited me to lunch for advice on how best to approach Dick Schulze for a gift. I asked how much they were considering asking for, and they indicated one to two million dollars.

Dick is a friend, and I didn't want to do him any disservice. I explained he was by nature a generous man with a great deal of class. There were two factors I considered significant to their gift request. First, I knew Dick felt the university didn't seem to acknowledge the business he had built in their backyard. Second, I knew Dick never had a chance to go to college but had achieved far more than the top one percent of our business school alumni. My suggestion was to give him an honorary doctorate and I thought they would be pleased by the manner in which he responded.

They didn't take my advice. Two years later, St. Thomas University, a local Jesuit school, awarded an honorary doctorate to Dick. His response? He gave $50 million plus $3.5 million for the Richard Schulze Endowed Chair in entrepreneurship. How's that for class and generosity?

Unfortunately, I have also experienced situations on boards that have made me extremely uncomfortable. On one board where I served as Chair of Compensation, the board was casting crucial votes about the compensation for the Chairman of the Board and the CEO that I did not support.

My positions in both cases were supported by recommendations from outside compensation consultants.

One way to ensure maximizing peer pressure is to sequence the roll call in the order that best serves the person taking the roll call (i.e., call on supporters first to pressure subsequent votes)—exactly what was done in both of the above cases. My position was well known and the Chairman of the Board called on me last. Besides feeling the full weight of peer pressure, I also knew that a no vote would not change the outcome and I would be in a losing minority.

No problem—I voted no each time. Why? Well, I learned from my misconduct as an undergraduate student in the accounting class. I also did not want peer pressure to drive me to a decision I didn't consider to be in the best interest of the shareholders.

In Chapter 1, we referenced the Enron scandal which is a powerful illustration of how peer pressure can conflict with inner compass and independence. For reading convenience the quote from

158

Professor Pfeffer about his colleague Professor Jaedicke is reprinted below:

The question posed by those who know Jaedicke well is how could this ethical, honest, and decent man have been caught up in such a massive financial fraud? There are many possible and plausible answers, including the fact that responsibility can become diffused when many people are present and observing an action (e.g., Latane and Darley, 1968), in that no single individual may feel particularly responsible or comfortable with disagreeing with the others.

In the case of the Chairman of the Board's compensation, the other two members of the Compensation Committee reversed their votes in favor of the Chairman. At this point in the roll call, there was only one no vote—from the Founder, former Chairman, and 10% stockholder, who for over a decade as Chairman refused additional compensation. He is a friend I greatly admire.

When I was asked to vote, I wasn't quite ready, so I said, "Can I think about it for just a moment?" As the meeting continued, I realized a no vote would make no difference and likely mean there would be a move by the Chairman to remove me as Chair of Compensation and likely off the Board: (I was right.) I drew upon my inner compass, whispered a little prayer, retained my independence and voted—NO.

There is a reason for the majority of the board to be independent directors (i.e., not current or recent employees). They are supposed to have other employment and not be financially dependent upon the income from being a board member. The theory is that financial independence encourages oversight independence. Sometimes that is not enough precaution if inner compasses lose their bearing.

After the meeting, I shared a limo to the airport with another board member and, ironically, a member of the Compensation Committee who had reversed his previous vote. As we drove off from corporate headquarters, he told me he actually agreed with my position on the Chairman's compensation—even though he voted against my recommendation. Up until that point, I considered him a friend that I admired. Do you think this gesture increased or decreased my admiration and trust of him as a friend?

I found it hard to believe I had hesitated for even a second to vote with the Founder but was more than pleased that I had.

Three Perspectives on Using an Erratic Compass – John

I have talked at great lengths with a man who is educated, articulate, sophisticated and very successful but whose standards are shallow. He has been in my home; I have been in his home. He is a man of incredible vision who can see the developments in his industry years ahead of his competition, and he reaps the financial rewards of being that sort of visionary. He is well known in his industry for treating customers with great fairness and business associates with impeccable honesty. He is deeply devoted to his employees and goes to great lengths to care for them. He is an impressive man by society's standards if one does not look too deeply.

At a glance, he seems like a well-grounded family man and businessman. But in reality, he doesn't have his inner compass properly set, nor does he have friends who mirror his behavior back to him. He regularly has been unfaithful to his wives (the first one left him for obvious reasons) and brags about the conquests he has made. It does not even bother him to gossip about men whom he considers his closest friends.

It is not hard to see the contradictions in this man's life. In his value system, it is not acceptable to cheat in business or short-change his vendors, but it is okay to cheat on his wife through his unfaithfulness. It is all right to cheat the government out of as much tax payment as he can. He bragged that he has created an art form out of sending cash through the mail to avoid a paper trail for taxation purposes. With his erratic compass, he could never allow himself to be dishonest with his customers, but he doesn't mind ruining the reputations of the women with whom he has had affairs (or, with whom he says he has had liaisons, because in some cases his boasting is known to be untrue), or to gossip about people and hurt them behind their backs.

He goes to great lengths to be equitable to people of all races and was gleefully proud that he beat the stuffing out of his young son when the kid made a derogatory remark about someone of a different color.

The reality is that the man does not have an inner compass that challenges him to a higher set of standards. He has a faulty and erratic inner compass. Thus, he is free to do whatever he wants to do, regardless of how it hurts other people. And he has no friends who are genuine enough in the relationship to evaluate his behavior for him and to tell him his behavior is wrong, or, if he does, perhaps he is ignoring them. I know when I tried to talk to him, I was dismissed as a nice guy who was a minister but does not understand life.

Unlike the man described above who has no compass, some create a bogus compass for themselves. For a second story, consider this. A couple of years ago, while on vacation, I was listening to an oldies but goodies rock-and-roll station. I was having a great time singing along with some of my long-time favorites when the DJ came back on. He said some very disparaging things about overweight high school girls who also struggle with acne.

That kind of comment hurts kids and also gives malicious and immature kids ammunition to make fun of one another. I telephoned the station to get his email address and actually was put through to him. I told him I was a minister and over the years have seen lots of high school kids deeply hurt by the kinds of words he was using on his show. His only response was, "I appreciate your call, Reverend, but I have been doing this for twenty five years," and he hung up.

161

What is his compass? Himself. Does he examine himself? Nope. He does not care if he hurts high school kids who struggle with their weight and complexion. The attitude of "it works and I am right" is the kind of attitude that keeps many of us from looking to Christ as our compass.

As a final story, others have the right compass but use it in the wrong way. I was sitting in a meeting with Christian leaders who were being quite self-congratulatory about how well Christian groups in that city worked together and supported one another.

Then I looked across the room and saw a college president who had not made a courtesy call or visit to a seminary president. He had failed to report that his school, which was only a few miles away, was beginning a competing seminary.

In my view, the man was not making certain that he was on course with how Christ would have led him. At the very least, I think Jesus Christ would have wanted the man to make a call to his fellow president to explain why he was starting a new seminary to avoid putting his counter-part in the awkward position of trying to explain to donors and friends of both schools what was taking place.

If we could peel back the layers of the onion in the man's mind and heart, we would find a man who wanted to follow Christ's inner compass. But because he did not surround himself with friends who would tell him the truth about his behavior, he sometimes followed an erratic compass. In other words, he probably had lots of acquaintances but not many, if any, real friends.

Again, we all have an inner compass. We just have to make certain the compass guiding us is true and not erratic. If it is erratic, we give ourselves the freedom to do and say what we want, without any sense of accountability to anyone or any sense of responsibility to the people we use, misuse or hurt.

Or we do not follow Christ's inner compass as closely as we would like and do not always act in a Christ-like way. Without Christ's inner compass, we will not grow as people, nor will we achieve what Christ wants us to achieve. If our inner compass is erratic, we probably do not have enough friends in our lives to tell us the truth. Achieving a High Performance Friendship is guaranteed by using a good inner compass.

Christ's Approach to Independence and Inner Compass

In this chapter, we have used the term inner compass in a number of different ways. We believe God does put knowledge of Himself in our hearts and minds at birth, and it is our decision as to whether we respond to Him. Jesus said He is "the way, the truth and the life" and therefore He is the ultimate inner compass. In the context of this book, He should be the inner compass guiding us to meaningful friendships—His kind of friendships. Since Christ is indeed the ultimate inner compass, it follows that no one can live life to the fullest, enjoy friendship, or be the kind of friend Christ desires us to be without a properly oriented inner and moral compass.

For our compasses to guide us properly, we must make a commitment to the absolute truth of the Bible as our one true guide for life. Of equal importance, we must constantly be evaluating ourselves against that inner compass—which we know is truth and grace since that is how Jesus lived. And we must have friends who are willing to evaluate us and tell us about our blind spots. We see this in Jesus: He was always motivated to honor God the Father. Thus He said His sustenance was to do the will of the Father. In this spirit, He was constantly pointing out ways for His followers to become better people when He saw their attitudes or behavior did not honor the Father.

Many people say they are followers of Christ but still lead lives of great inconsistency. The problem is not with the standards set by Christ, but with those who pick and choose when and how they follow His compass. This is why the Apostle Paul's words are so profound when he writes that we are to bring every thought subject to the obedience of Christ—the one true compass for life. This is not about knowing about Christ, but becoming more Christ-like in all we do. This is a life-long process. Just as it does us no good to know about Jesus without personally knowing Him, it does us no good to know His teachings but not apply them to our daily lives.

In the Sermon on the Mount, Jesus said, "Blessed are the poor in spirit, for theirs is the kingdom of heaven." It is not easy to think of ourselves in terms such as "poor." But in this context, Jesus uses the word "poor" to mean being spiritually destitute, being aware of our need for God to be working in our lives and being aware of what God requires of us if we are to see His kingdom. Jesus' meaning is clear. He is saying, "Blessed are those who recognize they are destitute and impoverished when it comes to any spiritual ability or capability. These are the ones who will see My kingdom." This truth is very applicable to the inner compass of friendship. Jesus is asking us to assess ourselves honestly and admit where we fall short of walking according to His compass.

If we cannot admit our shortcomings and we always have to be right, we do not have an attitude of spiritual poverty. Spiritual poverty is not a weakness; it is a strength. And that strength comes from our admission that we need Christ's power in our lives. Jesus is talking about the inner self, about our absolute need to admit we cannot guide ourselves through life using our own flawed inner compasses.

This truth is very applicable to the inner compass of friendship. Jesus was asking us to assess ourselves honestly and admit where we fall short of walking according to His compass. It is not easy to acknowledge our inadequacy. We do not like admitting we lack the character to live as Jesus the Lord lived. But Jesus is telling us the person who makes this admission is blessed, meaning he or she prospers spiritually and emotionally at the hand of God. Step Four of Alcoholics Anonymous gives a good explanation of this great truth when it says, "Make a searching and fearless moral inventory of ourselves." Such introspection is needed in all our lives, not just in the lives of addicts.

Jesus helps us understand spiritual poverty with His words "Apart from Me you can do nothing." Indeed, apart from the empowerment of Christ, we can do nothing to be Christ-like. We have absolutely nothing to offer the Holy God, the Creator of everything around us. And unless our inner compasses are fixed firmly on Him, we can never be in the process of learning how to live the way He wants us to in any area of our lives.

An anonymous writer explains Jesus' perspective of spiritual impoverishment this way:

"During my days of being an agnostic and then my early days of inquiry into Christian faith, I was not aware of my sin. In lifestyle I was not much different than the average churchgoer. In my own estimation, I was a pretty decent fellow. But when I realized that Christ was perfect and I was not, I began to understand how He viewed me. I was imperfect; I was sinful; that is why He died for my sins. At that point I understood what being poor in spirit means. I was not to compare myself to others; I was to compare myself to Christ and I came up very short."

Following Christ as our inner compass is acknowledging His perfection, His being "the way, truth and the life," admitting our imperfections, letting friends point out needed areas of growth and then asking God to change our lives.

Principles of Independence and Inner Compass

There are genuine and good friendships outside of being a Christ-follower. The difference is that friendships guided by Jesus' inner compass are tougher and more edifying. Since Christ's compass is the standard for friendship, there has to be a mutual commitment, not only to those standards, but also to letting each other suggest mid-course corrections for improvement.

As Lou Holtz, the famous football coach says, there have to be three dynamics:

1. Do you *care* about me?
2. Do you *trust* me?
3. Do we *share the same values*?

Both players in a friendship must have the same value of wanting to become conformed to the image of Jesus Christ or there will always be something lacking in the friendship.

The man with the erratic compass mentioned above, who would never cheat at business but cheats on his wife, does not claim to be a follower of Christ. But what about those who do say Jesus is their inner compass? Is there a difference in how they relate to friends? A great many people say they are followers of Christ but they still lead lives of great inconsistency. The problem is not with the standard set by Christ, but with those who pick and choose when and how they follow His standards; they are using Jesus as the inner compass only when it is convenient for them.

John saw a bumper sticker that read, "Damn! I'm good." It seems as though the driver of this car sets his own standard. We live in a society that places great value on achievement, self-esteem, and personal strength. This does not make for a spiritual climate conducive to admitting spiritual poverty. But Jesus tells us self-examination and honesty are the first steps in acknowledging our absolute inability to live for Him and our need for His compass.

Jesus-style friendships do not happen naturally—we have to want such friendships. Many men lack the ability or willingness to do any self-reflection. Self-reflection is tough. Self-evaluation and letting others evaluate us takes maturity, honesty and a willingness to admit we do not measure up to the standards of Christ to grow the way we should.

For some, it is just easier to settle into an easy Christianity and evaluate ourselves against other imperfect people or our own Christian subculture. Someone once said, "People become part and parcel of the Christian subcultures in which they are immersed." We do not know of any such cultures that tolerate drunkenness or sexual sins but we know plenty that tolerate meetings after meetings instead of face-to-face honesty, that tolerate gossip and slander and even plenty that tolerate the unkindness (some would call it rudeness) of not returning phone calls, emails, etc. It is easy—even in Christian organizations and churches—to utilize a substandard compass. But when we use Jesus Christ as our inner compass, we grow. Sometimes it hurts. The book of Hebrews tells us that God disciplines the ones He loves.

We know of a situation where pastors in a group complained about a fellow pastor who criticized some of them, their theology and their churches. Then one day, he came into the group and nothing was said about it. When one of the men was asked about this lack of love shown toward this man, he said, "The issue of criticism never came up." Not caring enough to raise the issue or to help our friends grow seems to be a grievous lack of caring and is insincere friendship.

It seems the proof of a commitment to Christ's inner compass is that we are willing to be corrected by others and we are willing to correct others. Dale Carnegie said most people are reluctant to admit they are wrong and are reluctant to take criticism. Yet Ralph Waldo Emerson said, "Let me never fall into the vulgar mistake of dreaming that I am persecuted whenever I am contradicted." But as has been stated by many, "If you care, you correct"—so a friend resisting correction is not a good enough reason to back away from him.

Herb Gregg, an acquaintance of John, spent many years as an overseas missionary and provides a compelling perspective on inner compass. Muslim extremists kidnapped Herb and held him for eight months in Makhachkala, Dagestan, in the former Soviet Union. During his time in captivity, Herb never left his cell, a small room without running water, toilet or bed. He was never allowed to change his clothes and on no fewer than one hundred occasions, he was threatened with death.

Some months after Herb's release, he said, "I had been an active missionary for thirty-three years. In prison, I was still for an extended period of time. Then God began to pinpoint sins and sin patterns in my life. Specifically, He pinpointed a lack of love toward my sister. I started to weep. Until that point in my life, my heart was too hard to weep over my sins."

As we consider deeply what Herb said, we realize he had learned something far beyond our understanding and experience. He had learned that although he had spent all those years serving God, he still needed to confess his sins, imperfections and inconsistencies before his inner compass could point more directly to God. He was not his own standard—Jesus Christ was his standard. Herb's story illustrates that when we are constantly setting our own inner compasses toward Jesus Christ, we see areas where we need repentance and spiritual growth. While we are imperfect, God is perfect in all He thinks, says, and does.

This is the God before whom we must humble ourselves and acknowledge our spiritual impoverishment. Once we do that, He is willing to bless and benefit us in ways we can only imagine.

Discussion Questions and Applications

1. How do we decide what our inner compass is going to be, and how do we make sure it is not an erratic compass?

2. Jim and John obviously disagree on the use of tests in college. Regardless of your disagreement with either one, comment on their ability to discuss the issue within the context of two friends who obviously hold each other in such high regard.

3. Do you think that a huge transgression like Enron starts with becoming comfortable with small transgressions and graduating to higher level ones?

4. How do we determine what is a value and what is an absolute truth?

5. Why do we elevate our values to the level of an absolute truth?

6. We all understand and have experienced peer pressure. How do we avoid succumbing to negative peer pressure?

7. How do we as Christian men make certain that our faith in Christ is not academic but indeed an inner compass on which we are relying in every area of our life?

8. Spiritual poverty and admitting that without Christ we can do nothing are hard truths to admit. Why is this so?

9. Do you agree that an integral part of being led by an inner compass is having friends who are honest and care enough to tell us the truth about ourselves?

10. What stories about inner compass could you share with your friends in a helpful manner?

Chapter 9

Kindness

What do we live for, if it is not to make life less difficult for each other?
~ *George Eliot*

It is easier to forgive an enemy than to forgive a friend.
~ *William Blake*

Some additional quotes regarding kindness:

There is nothing we like to see so much as the gleam of pleasure in a person's eye when he feels that we have sympathized with him, understood him. At these moments something fine and spiritual passes between two friends. These are the moments worth living.
~ *Don Marquis*

As I observe my life from my death bed, I have come to the conclusion that I have not done one good thing for anyone else.
~ *Randall Beeler*

The quote by Beeler above is a heartbreaking way for one to look back on a life. Kindness among friends pertains to benevolence, considerateness and helpfulness—it is a pleasure of high performance friendships. It usually takes our maturing to learn that it is truly better to give than to receive. The deep sense of well being that comes from helping a friend in kindness is truly amazing. And it provides us the opportunity to look back upon a life that is fulfilling and that made a difference.

Have you ever noticed how friendship can work like a mirror? When we are kind and thoughtful to others, we tend to stimulate that response from others. Conversely, if we are selfish and thoughtless, we stimulate those responses from others?

Here is an illustration. Let's say you and a friend are deciding on a movie or a restaurant. One person expresses a strong desire for his choice, which his friend dislikes. If they don't agree on either choice, arguing might follow. As each one becomes more insistent, the other tends to resist even more (i.e., like a mirror). Sometimes the two, in an effort to win, start recalling who got to decide last time and the time before, etc. If one person prevails and gets his way, the other belligerently acquiesces and often complains about anything negative associated with experiencing that choice (e.g., "I hope you are enjoying the movie; did you even check the reviews on this before you forced it on me?"). Sometimes people even hope that the choice turns out negatively to prove they were right all along.

On the other hand, if two friends are disputing the choice for a movie or a restaurant and one suddenly acquiesces in a cooperative manner that can change everything. Suppose one friend says, "You know it doesn't matter so much where we go. The important thing is for us to share a good time together. Let's go with your choice."

Have you noticed when that kind gesture is offered, it tends to mirror a response of, "You're right, I am being unreasonable, let's go with your choice." Often at this point, the conversation reverses from each person insisting upon their own choice to insisting on the other's choice.

Kindness begets kindness.

That having been said, an art to kindness is to avoid the trap of enabling. Some people take advantage of a kind friend and may become dependent, knowing that the friend picks up the slack (e.g., they do not return a loan or let the friend always pay the check at restaurants).

When Jim was on the faculty at the University of Memphis, he had a conversation with someone who had observed a dynamic of Elvis

Presley's relationship with his friends. His friends were like leeches who always had their hands out for big ticket items—like cars—which Elvis bought for many of his friends. He said someone once asked, "Doesn't Elvis realize they are using him?" The answer was, "Yes, but those are the only friends he has." Sad.

Jim did a revealing experiment at an amusement park. Three boys were longingly looking at a huge slide they obviously wanted to ride. Jim went over and purchased some tickets and offered one to each of the three boys. In grateful disbelief, they took them, and after a thrilling experience returned and collectively said, "Thank you so much!" Jim offered three more tickets and asked if they would like to go again. They enthusiastically squealed yes and were off again. The cycle was repeated several times. Eventually, the boys, in their rush to get back in line, would run past Jim and grab the tickets—expressions of gratitude had evaporated.

Finally, on after what would be the final run, the boys were told there were no more tickets. They expressed dismay and asked if more could be purchased. They were told, "Sorry, but no." Now the three boys, who had been diminishing in gratitude after each subsequent ride, were a choir of groaning disappointment. They made another appeal but were told, "The tickets are all gone." They walked away not even saying thank you for what was initially highly appreciated.

The quote from Randall Beeler above continues to haunt John. He was a neighbor of John's parents in the neighborhood where John was raised. It was the kind of neighborhood where anyone's parents could swat or discipline anyone's kids—and the parents would support the neighbor. Mr. Beeler was very reflective as he lay on his deathbed. The quote above is from a letter he wrote to John as he was dying. It is hard to imagine a person evaluating the entirety of his life and realizing he had not done "one good thing." Kindness brings great satisfaction to the giver; selfishness does not bring joy. It is better to give than to receive.

Kindness is a beautiful gesture but also a balancing act. Jesus demonstrated it when he healed the lepers and only one bothered to return to be thankful. Gratefulness and reciprocity are the other bookend of kindness.

Kind Heart – Jim

A rewarding aspect of being an author is that people often ask you what you are working on. As you share your current project, people often provide helpful perspectives or experiences that are constructive to the book or article. I had a business lunch the other day, and Achieving High Performance Friendship became a topic of discussion. After lunch Phil one of the men, pulled me aside in the parking lot. He shared a profound experience with me that he kindly gave me permission to share with you.

He explained that several years ago he had to have quadruple bypass surgery. As part of the hospital discharge protocol, he was asked to fill out a survey. One of the questions on the survey asked if he had a friend he could talk to. Without much thought, he checked off No. He asked and found out that the answer to that question was a significant predictor of recovery.

Later, he mentioned that to a casual friend. In response, the casual friend started calling Phil every morning at 9 a.m., like clockwork, to see how he was doing. Out of kindness, this soon to be deep friend made himself available to let Phil share whatever was on his mind. As Phil told me the story, he put his hand on his chest and with watery eyes said, "You know Jim, each time he called and we talked, I swear I could feel healing in my heart."

Phil went on to say that years later he was involved in a personal development exercise that involved writing letters of appreciation to the most significant people in his life. He, of course, wrote this friend. A few days later, his friend called and said, "Phil, I have read your letter five times and every time I break down and cry. Thank you for the letter and for being my friend."

A beautiful story that so clearly demonstrates how we benefit by developing high performance friendships.

Once we learn that it is indeed more blessed to give than to receive, we have the opportunity to learn that gratitude can mean more to the giver than the gift of kindness did to the receiver.

Kindness Does Not Depend on Circumstances – John

I am a great believer in the research into birth order. By some studies, I am the classic middle child: competitive, mouthy and cocky. So the Holy Spirit has had a major league job working to conform me to the image of Christ as it relates to kindness—and He has a lot more work to do.

These birth order qualities have not always stood me in good stead with people in authority when they chose to be disrespectful or acerbic. The malady started early in life. My freshman year in high school, I gave a smart-aleck response to a teacher who thought she needed to tell me I was not the student my brother was. (He graduated in the spring and I entered in the fall.) I was surprised it took her ten weeks to figure that out. So I confess (remember, "Confession is good for the soul, but bad for the reputation") that I have had to do some deep and penetrating self-examination as I continue to learn about kindness being one aspect of the Fruit of the Spirit.

I have had the privilege of training pastors in countries where democracy has not been honored and autocrats rule. Men who live by the inner compass of Christ in two of the countries have had a huge impact on me as I have observed their responses of kindness to authorities who have been less than respectful to them. One country is Romania and the other cannot be named for security reasons.

Nicolae Ceausescu, the former Secretary General of the Communist Party in Romania, said "the poplar trees in the parks of Bucharest would grow pears before Romania became a democratic country." To mock Ceausescu's words after he was overthrown, the university students in Bucharest went to the parks and hung pears from the poplar trees to add insult to injury.

Pastor David knew the secret police were in his church services every Sunday. He had Bibles buried under the basement of the church, and they were given out only after David discerned that the person was a sincere believer in Christ. He knew his phone was tapped.

Pastor David, as all pastors in Romania unless they compromised with the government, lived under perpetual scrutiny and suspicion. David knew he was followed constantly.

While we were walking together down the street one day, I started to ask him a question. He stopped me gently with these words spoken in his charming and broken English, "Brudder John, we will talk later." When we talked later, he explained directional microphones to me. Such microphones could pick up our conversations from hundreds of yards away.

Another time, one of the hosts of one of our seminars for pastors was killed by the secret police, who stuck a poison dart on the end of an umbrella into his back at a train station.

Yet I never heard David complain about these secret police. He lamented their station in life. On one of my visits, I brought a letter from our U.S. Senator along with gifts for the mayor of the city. David took the letter and the gifts to the mayor and asked him to see me. An hour or so later, David returned to his office—with a look of disbelief and incredulity on his face. He said, "Brudder John, he is afraid to see you. He is the prisoner; I am a free man. I feel sorry for him." David's attitude was much more Christ-like than mine was.

Another pastor in a nearby city, Pastor Alexander, told me that after the revolution overthrowing Nicolae Ceausescu, a secret policeman came to him to apologize and ask his forgiveness. He said to Alexander, "I have always known you were a good man. I was only doing my duty as a soldier." I saw sympathy and compassion for the secret policeman in Pastor Alexander, not the resentment that I would have felt.

I have seen the same attitude among church leaders in the country I cannot name. The church is outlawed. Training pastors is illegal. I must confess I have a knot in my stomach whenever I am there. It is rewarding, but not fun, to have to show up in the dark of very early morning to the place where I am teaching and not leave until the dark of night because the pastors are being watched. Yet I see the same thing I saw in Romania. The pastors do not complain; they feel sorry for the secret police. They treat them with kindness.

One friend was detained for eleven hours. When the interrogation was over, he said, "These police officers have been treated with respect by other pastors they have detained. I can tell by how they have treated us. Their detaining us is the only way they ever get the opportunity to hear that God loves them."

One man even went to the police who were sitting in their car outside his house because they were trailing him 24/7. He told them he was not going anywhere that night and they should go home to see their children. They told him they could not do that and then said, "If you ever need a ride, please let us know."

One secret police officer even showed up at a pastor's home and told the pastor he was volunteering to teach the officer's men about marriage from the Bible. He said words to the effect, "My men are not effective in their jobs because of their poor marriages. I know you are teaching on marriage and I want you to come to help me help my men."

As I am learning from these men, kindness is not dependent on the circumstances. These men have manifested a kindness that is courteous and respectful.

The kindness these courageous men manifest causes the pastors to wonder what circumstances in life have forced the persons with whom they are interacting to be as rude, ungracious and selfish as they are. Thus, they do not feel humiliated by the secret police but feel compassion for them. Christ-followers are to live above the circumstances. I know how to preach and teach on the subject of kindness—but learning to live it is a life-long journey. These good men and dear brothers do not deny the disrespectful treatment they have received, or still get, but they were/are following the inner compass of Christ that says we are to be people of kindness.

They did not know their spiritually mature behavior was shaming me, because my inclination was to want to figure out how to fight back, instead of following the inner compass of Christ. I am a better person for having had their influence in my life. I understand more about kindness from watching them live out kindness under tough circumstances.

Cruel to Be Kind – Jim

I have had financial success in my career not so much from being a professor but through business books, consulting and speaking. It has its advantages and disadvantages. An advantage is that you can be kind and helpful to friends. The disadvantage is that giving money just because someone needs it is not always helpful or appreciated. Friends know I am able to help them financially and can be resentful when for good reason I am not willing.

Interestingly, one of my best friends, Ronnie, from high school, provided perspective that was accurate, surprising and helpful. I had always been willing to hold a job—sometimes two or three at a time. I had learned the lesson of saving money for a rainy day. Friends would often borrow from me with promises and, I believe, intent to pay it back. They often were late. They would put me in the unpleasant position of asking for it. Sometimes, I would learn they had made other purchases rather than honoring the commitment to return the loan.

Here was Ronnie's simple but apparently accurate explanation. He said, "Jim, you have to understand when your friends borrow from you, they know you are loaning them money you don't really need; otherwise you wouldn't be able to make the loan in the first place." Ronnie continued, "If it creates a hardship for them to pay you back, well, again it wasn't money you really needed, so they were not creating a hardship for you."

I couldn't believe it at the time. I do now.

I have helped many friends where the help was not in their best interest, and the outcome deeply hurt both of us.

I have a childhood friend who is in the home construction business that was wiped out during the savings and loan crises in the 1990's. As a favor, I invested with him in a land deal that, if it worked out as he promised, would allow him to financially recover and would get me a good return on my investment. Ultimately, we made a good return...but it took twice as long as promised—however, that wasn't the problem.

Without elaborating, he did not keep his word and created a situation where I had to incur more expense for the project to survive. Though he had created the problem and I was forced to financially resolve it, he wanted me to cover half of the expense out of the proceeds when we sold the project. He argued that we were partners and therefore should share all expenses, regardless of the source. As a silent and favor-providing partner, I felt he should accept full responsibility for his mistake and for putting me in a financial bind.

Here's the choice I gave him. Since you can't cover the expense I will cover it for now. When we sell, you can reimburse me in full or, alternatively, you can maintain that I should pay for half of the expense for the problem you created. To resolve our conflict, I will honor your choice, but please know that if you chose the latter, I will no longer consider you a trusted friend. He chose the latter, and the friendship evaporated. He approached me two more times, pleading with me to invest in another deal with him. He argued that I had actually, in the end, made a good return. It didn't matter—he had established his priorities. To back him again would not have been kind to him or me. I felt I had to be cruel to be kind so that he would understand the value of a friendship versus the value of money.

Several times I have given friends in financial need a nice late-model vehicle of their choice free and clear. Can you imagine my hurt and disappointment when some of them later used the gift as a down payment to buy a new vehicle they couldn't afford? And of course, when they couldn't make the payment, who did they think should bail them out again? When I refused in an effort to help them grow by being cruel to be kind, I later learned they com-plained to other friends that I was too selfish to help a friend.

But let's consider a story where kindness was more than rewarded. Jamin is a younger friend of mine—actually a nephew by marriage. He was brought up in a Jehovah's Witness family, where education is not viewed favorably. He is the only one of four brothers who graduated from high school.

He ultimately chose against being a Jehovah's Witness and was excommunicated from his family and church friends. He married my niece Cassie at a young age and worked construction but, due to injuries sustained at work, really needed a different career direc-tion. At the time, Jamin was thirty and he and Cassie had three children.

Jamin had done some work for me, and he always impressed me as sincere and hard working. He just needed a break. I offered to help financially if he wanted to start college. He indicated he had always wanted to be an engineer—not an easy field of study. But he also explained that with his family obligations, he wasn't sure how he could return the favor. I told him I thought he had not been given a fair opportunity and he could repay me by working hard, making good grades and helping out someone younger than he someday.

At thirty-five, five years later, Jamin graduated with a 4.16 (that's right, higher than an A average) in chemical engineering. At the time of writing this book he was being hotly pursued for graduate school and science jobs in government and industry. His class-mates all recommended he become a professor.

Who do you think feels most rewarded for a kind gesture?

I was so honored when he called me after he was offered a full-ride scholarship and a prestigious internship with an impressive salary to pursue a PhD. He said, "I called you first because I wanted you to know and knew you would provide the best advice."

I couldn't be more proud of Jamin if he were my own son.

Kindness in the Midst of the Killing Fields – John

For the past nine years, I have spent a lot of time in Burundi in Central Africa. While 1,000,000 people were being slaughtered in Rwanda, 250,000 people were being slaughtered in Burundi—not for the color of their skin, not for political convictions—only because of who their great, great grandmothers were—either of the Tutsi tribe or the Hutu tribe.

I have stood in the killing fields. I have seen the empty homes—empty because all the inhabitants were killed. I have helped raise money for an orphanage building to house the surviving children. I have friends who have had family members slaughtered. I lost a good friend to murder (seven bullets to the head) because he was a leader in the reconciliation process. The stories go on and on… and are forever etched in my mind and soul. But the stories that still haunt me the most are these:

Rebels stopped a caravan of cars and told the 12 people to get out and lie down on the ground. The rebels were going to shoot them only because they all were Tutsis. Along came a Catholic priest who was a Hutu. He perceived what was happening, got out of his car and lay down in the middle of the Tutsis. When the rebels told him to move, he said, "No, we are neither Hutu nor Tutsi, we are Burundians. What you do to these, you have to do to me." His courageous act caused enough confusion that someone was able to call United Nations soldiers nearby, and the rebels scattered. Jesus said, "There is no greater love than to lay down your life for your friends."

One day, I was walking in a town square with one of my translators. I did not recognize who he saw but he said, "Brother John, it is difficult to walk in town and see the people who killed my family." I asked, "Sebastian, how do you do it? How do you move forward in life? How do you live without resentment?" He said, very respectfully, as though I should know the answer, "Brother John, you ask Jesus for the power to forgive, and you move on. You cannot be controlled by anger. Life is about serving others."

My friends took me to a Catholic seminary surrounded by a high stone wall. Nearby was a hill from which rebels had lobbed shells into the seminary compound. Then they had busted in with machine guns drawn. They had ordered the forty seminarians (all about the age of twenty) to separate by tribe, "Tutsi over there, Hutu over here." The implication was clear. The Tutsis would be murdered; the Hutus would be spared. One by one, these brave young men had said, "We are not Hutu or Tutsi...we are Burundian." They had refused to move. The rebels killed them all. Here I was at the chapel where their grave site is. I looked at forty headstones...with different birth dates and one death date. I looked at a painting of all their faces on the wall of the chapel. I was stunned. My translator on this occasion wept. I could not talk. I could not move. I could hardly breathe because the lump in my throat was so large.

I thought back to being a twenty-year-old sophomore in a fraternity house at the University of Oregon and wondered if I would have refused to move for the men with whom I lived...knowing I would be killed if I did not move. I had to confess to God and myself that

I would have moved. Interestingly, the cemetery where these forty heroes are buried is called "The Fraternity of the Martyrs."

On one of my trips I wrote an email to some friends from high school days. This is an abbreviated version of what I wrote after visiting a memorial for some high school kids:

I am in Burundi where I have finished speaking. I leave for Kenya tomorrow. I have been traveling here to speak for nine years. I thought I had heard enough and seen enough that I sort of understood the depths of the pain. I have read about 5000 pages on the killings here and in Rwanda. This morning I am in the capital city of Bujumbura. We were driven back here from Gitega, the second largest city in Burundi, where a colleague and I had spoken at a pastors' conference.

On the way, we stopped at a memorial. It is particularly poignant as many of us will soon be together for a reunion at our high school back in Oregon. This memorial commemorates the killing of two hundred students in one school by their headmaster, who was a Hutu. When the genocide started he had some goons/soldiers/rebels with machetes herd all two hundred Tutsi students into two rooms of a stone building. They were jammed tightly together in these two small rooms—which still stand at the memorial—standing back to chest and side to side. Doors were locked and gasoline was poured in and ignited, and the kids were burned to death. I cannot imagine the horror those kids felt. I stood in the rooms trying to think of the screaming, panic, fear, smell of burning flesh, etc. I simply could not get my mind around it.

I thought of some of you. Would I have tried, along with other football players, to fight back? Would we have tried to comfort one another? Obviously, one cannot know. I tried to think of our principal, Dr. Burgess, doing this to us. He was such a good man that my mind could not even start down that track of thinking. I tried to think what the Hutu kids who were not herded into the two rooms might feel fifty years later when/if they have a reunion as we are preparing to have at our school. I became so angry at the memorial I thought I could kill the headmaster myself—with my bare hands. Thankfully, he was tracked down and executed by the government after he ran from the area. I assume parents would have found him and done the same if the government had not done it.

Well, anyway, I just wanted to share this with you. I am so glad we did not have to live through something like what the memorialized kids experienced. And, although I will never know, I hope I would have been brave enough to try to protect those of you who were smaller and more vulnerable than I. Some of you I have known since we were in the first grade. I am glad I know you.

Jesus was described as "a man of sorrows and acquainted with grief" because of what He had to endure as the God/man to suffer for the sins of the world. Some of the men I have met in Burundi have a weightiness, a look about them that speaks of being men of sorrows. It is no wonder with all the killing they have seen...and the loss they have experienced. Yet, in spite of that pain and anguish, they talk about reconciliation. They do not live in the past. They pray for their former enemies. Their decision to live in kindness has challenged me to evaluate my lack of kindness. Ironically, I am invited here to serve and teach them...but I always leave being the one who was taught and helped.

High Performance Friendships are friendships of kindness.

Christ's Approach to Kindness

God is kindness. He expressed this kindness to us through Christ coming to earth as the God/man to serve and rescue us from our sin.

Jesus' greatest expression of kindness was manifested when He was being crucified. His concern for others did not diminish in spite of the pain He was experiencing. The Roman soldiers crucifying Him were trained killers...and they had elevated crucifixion to the most painful death imaginable. In the midst of all this pain, Jesus asked the Father to forgive His executioners; He promised one of the thieves dying with Him that he would be with Him in heaven; and He directed the Apostle John to care for His mother as his own. Kindness is caring for others.

Kindness is one aspect of the Fruit of the Spirit, which we understand is the clearest picture of Christ-like qualities. Actually, kindness and goodness go hand-in-hand. Kindness is the outward expression of a heart filled with goodness that wants others to get better, grow and improve. Kindness is the more gracious and pleasant way to help; kindness is a gentle expression of God's love. Goodness can be tougher but it is not nasty; goodness can rebuke and discipline. Goodness can be a more firm expression of God's love and standards. Jesus expressed kindness to the sinful woman who anointed His feet with her tears and wiped them with her hair. On the other hand He expressed goodness when He cleansed the temple.

In both descriptions of Jesus, we see His commitment to telling the truth and challenging people to live by His inner compass. It is important to remember that Jesus is "the way, truth and life." Thus, the Christ-like life is not a life of doing whatever we want but living as Christ lived when He was on earth.

Kindness is being truthful, helping, serving and inspiring others to improve. We see these qualities in Jesus as He ministered on earth. As His followers, we are to reflect Who He was when He was here.

Solomon talks about this attitude of helping others when he writes that the man who is kind to the needy will be blessed.

We understand Christ was a great teacher—the greatest in all of history. Much of His teaching was not in what He said but in how He acted or responded to people and situations. Thus, we learn a great deal about kindness by observing some of His gestures of kindness.

When the woman caught in adultery was brought to Him, He did not shame her, but He did expose her accusers as hypocrites. He talked to her about forgiveness and leading a pure life in the future…and asked her accusers to look into their own dirty hearts to acknowledge their own sinfulness.

When He healed ten lepers and only one came back to thank Him, He seemed surprised. Indeed, He asked rhetorically, "Did I not heal ten?" But He did not hurl verbal abuse at them. He was kind and let the obvious message stand alone: be thankful when people help you. He was always kind to outcasts. He did not walk away from them as we have learned to do with our eyes diverted and our body language portraying that we want to be left alone.

When the woman with an issue of blood snuck through the crowd to touch the hem of His robe, He stopped His procession to ask who had touched Him. She was afraid but He drew her in. He affirmed her; He was not content to let her be healed by touching His garment. He gave her dignity through His kind response to her.

Jesus did not speak as much on kindness as He lived kindness— He taught by example. We can learn volumes about kindness from studying Him. The Apostle John said He was full of grace and truth. Both qualities are integral components of kindness.

Principles of Kindness

Kindness, as one part of the Fruit of the Spirit, is not based on circumstances. The follower of Christ must continually ask himself if he is controlled by circumstances or continuing to give himself to others.

As we learn from our brothers in other countries who have suffered incredible loss or disrespect, the power of Christ living in us can motivate and empower us to hope and pray for the spiritual well-being of those people.

Jesus said that apart from Him we can do nothing. The thought of being kind to those who have hurt us is a good example of how He wants to work in our lives.

Kindness is a very helpful teaching and correcting tool. Jesus often taught and corrected by using a question. Is it kinder to say, "Here is what you need to do." or "Are you open to a suggestion?" Is it kinder to say, "You are not being fair." or "Do you consider that fair?"

The phrase, "I will not regret my past nor seek to change it" can be helpful to us. It does not mean we ignore the past; rather, it means we focus on what we can achieve and accomplish in the future. Kindness is not milquetoast; it is strength. Kindness does not pre-clude building barriers to protect ourselves from someone who would hurt us. But kindness does not allow us to seek revenge. When kindness is manifested between two friends, they bring out the best in one another. They do not engage in putdowns or one-upmanship. Kind friends want the best for each other at all times. As stated above, kindness has a mirroring effect—we often stimu-late in others what we are to them.

Discussion Questions and Applications

1. Do we honestly love a person if we are unwilling to show them the tough love of goodness they might need?

2. We all have been hurt or cheated by someone in our lives. How do we apply Jesus' words that "apart from Me you can do noth-ing" to make sure we live lives of kindness?

3. We live in a society that seems not to be as kind as it used to be. How do we make sure we are being Christ-like regardless of society's values?

4. Let's think about our friendships. Do we communicate to our friends in kindness when they need to be corrected, or do we

just speak however we want? Do we care that we might back them into a corner and cause them to be defensive and closed-minded as opposed to speaking so they can receive what we need to say to them?

5. Think about when you needed to be corrected and someone did so in a kind manner. How did you feel and what did you think about that correction?

6. Jesus was full of grace and truth. How do these qualities help us understand kindness?

7. Following the mirroring principle, think of a time when you mirrored kindness and when you did not mirror kindness. What were the results?

8. We have read in this chapter about some people in other countries who have learned to live in kindness in spite of some very difficult and painful circumstances. What can we learn from them about our own lives and how we should manifest kindness?

9. Can you convert these statements to questions and see if they seem more kind? You need to help with the dishes. I need to speak to you. Don't be late. You have an attitude problem. You are not being nice. You are rude. You are gossiping.

10. We can actually make anything we want to say to someone a question, can't we?

11. What stories of kindness can you share in a helpful manner with your friends?

Chapter 10

Encouragement and Eternal Values

The glory of friendship is not the outstretched hand, nor the kindly smile, nor the joy of companionship; it is the spiritual inspiration that comes to one when you discover that someone else believes in you and is willing to trust you with a friendship. (adapted)
~ Ralph Waldo Emerson

When a friend is in trouble, don't annoy him by asking if there is anything you can do. Think up something appropriate and do it.
~ Edgar Watson Howe

To encourage a friend is to inspire with courage, spirit or confidence, often when we are feeling challenged or even overwhelmed and our emotional and spiritual tanks are empty. Encouragement from a friend during these times is invaluable as a primary benefit of a high performance friendship.

Ironically, when we are in our most difficult times—especially those we have brought upon ourselves—we are often not much of a friend to ourselves. There is a powerful way to encourage a friend or yourself when unhealthy self-criticism and deprecation is problematic. Psychologists recommend a simple exercise. Pretend your very best friend just made the same mistake and created the same problem. Think what you would say to him to encourage him. Then be sure you are being as encouraging to yourself as you would be to him.

Here is another powerful way we can encourage a friend or ourselves when we are a victim of circumstances beyond our control (e.g., a major betrayal from a friend or a catastrophic event that has occurred.) In this situation, the psychologists' advice is to pretend that our life is a story where something horrible has happened. We then take control as the author of our story and write the ending so that we end up a hero.

This is exactly what John did after discovering his child had become addicted to heroin. He authored and edited a book, **Hit by a Ton of Bricks**, created a radio ministry that plays on over four hundred radio stations and created the web site *www.notalone.org* which receives thousands of visits a year. Both the radio program and the website provide guidance and encouragement to parents who discover their children are abusing drugs or alcohol. John has constructively encouraged thousands of families through his ministry.

Encouragement mostly involves the thoughtfulness to say the right things at the right time. It is not so much about any enormous personal sacrifice. It usually requires little more than having a conversation to assure a friend that we believe in him and his ability to prevail or achieve in whatever his circumstance might be. It involves letting people know we care and believe in them.

Eternal Values work in perfect harmony with Encouragement. Sometimes, we can become so short-sighted and secular in our perspective that we lose sight that what really matters is what is eternal. Accordingly, when a friend is discouraged or fretting about making a difficult decision (e.g., career choice), we can be encouraging by asking, "When you consider this from Christ's eternal perspective, does that help and/or encourage you?"

If we do not share our discouragements with a friend, we need to grow more as a friend. And of course we are not much of a friend, let alone a high performance friend, if we are not paying enough attention to even realize a friend needs encouragement or we fail to encourage him, as illustrated in the first story below.

Anti-Encouragement – Jim

I worked my way through school without financial aid, scholarships or money from parents. School selection was determined by proximity and job opportunities. To be honest, my IQ scores wouldn't impress you as anything special. Whatever I have achieved has been through a willingness to work hard.

I went to New Mexico State University for an undergraduate business degree in systems analysis because it was nearby and I could get a job in the computer center. Texas Tech came next for graduate school because I was offered a job with NCR's Computer Division, and they would pay my tuition. I believe I was fortunate for the education I received, though no one would say I attended high-prestige universities. In retrospect, I am glad it worked out that way, as the socio-economic demographics of my classmates were similar to those of most Americans.

When I finished my PhD and went into the faculty job market, I asked my advisor for his recommendation of the best school for continuing my career. With no hesitation, he said, "Without a doubt, the University of Minnesota. They have the founding program and the premier PhD program."

In academia, we have job derbies at academic conferences where universities and new PhD's engage in something akin to a mating ritual to try to find a good match. I saw a professor from Minnesota whose name I recognized on his badge, and I was quite familiar with articles he had published. Uninhibited by my limitations I introduced myself, but found they were not hiring anyone that year.

I ended up taking a faculty position at the University of Houston, which was an ambitious up-and-coming university. They were recruiting people they perceived would work hard and help enhance their reputation.

After joining Houston, I had good fortune with my research and publishing. My books on Systems Analysis and Design were rated by *Computing Newsletter* as the best in the field, and I published articles in the top two journals.

As a result of the exposure from that success, three years later the University of Minnesota invited me to come speak to faculty and the business community in the Twin Cities. A few months later, they offered me a position at the University of Minnesota, which included a promotion from assistant to associate professor and the opportunity to direct their research center—the Management Information Systems Research Center. I was overwhelmed.

To properly consider the opportunity, I had a long conversation with a friend and senior professor at Houston who was in a significant leadership role. I sincerely sought his guidance on the advisability of making what would be a bold and challenging career move to the premier program in my field.

He did not offer encouragement. He said, "Jim, you have done well here at Houston. But don't delude yourself. A move to Minnesota puts you in the big leagues. What impresses your colleagues around here won't so easily impress colleagues with higher standards. I'm concerned you will be getting in over your head and not fare well in a much more competitive environment."

As the conversation continued, I paid close attention to the nuances of what he said and the motivation behind it. I sadly concluded that he was less concerned about objectively advising me than he was in simply convincing me to stay at Houston, as that better served his purposes. As I arrived at that conclusion, I lost trust in him as a friend and correctly discounted his advice.

I did join the faculty of the University of Minnesota and spent twenty wonderful years there—but not because someone I considered a friend encouraged me as he should have. He lost a colleague and a close friend because his encouragement was not genuine.

Loss of Legs but an Encourager Nonetheless – John

In a book about male friendships, I am including a story about a woman friend of mine. When asked why I would tell her story, the answer is simple. Her courage, faith and encouragement are so strong, in spite of her loss, that people cannot help but be encouraged by her.

I forget how the news came, but it came, and it was shocking news. My friend from high school, Dianne Gobel Meyer, had lost her legs due to medical malpractice. As soon as I could, I flew over to Las Vegas to see her and her husband, Ron. By the time I received the news, she was already walking on prosthetics. I was stunned to see her. I am not sure whether I hid my shock and emotions from her. I do know I went to Las Vegas to encourage her and ended up being the one who was encouraged.

The story in brief is that Ron, an FBI agent, took her to the hospital one night because she was very ill. She was told she had kidney stones, was given some pain medication and released to go home. She was told the pain medication would allow her to tolerate the pain of passing the stones.

Two days later, Ron returned her, deathly ill, to the hospital. What Ron and Dianne were not told was that an hour after they left the hospital, the staff looked at her blood tests again and saw that bile was in her blood stream. She should have been called and told to return to the hospital immediately–but she was not called. Indeed, the only reason she knew about the blood test was because a nurse risked her job later to tell Ron and Dianne about it. Amazingly, the doctor who initially treated Dianne denied seeing her in the hospital. But as an FBI agent, Ron did something which most of us would not have thought to do—he took copies of the hospital records with him when he left the hospital.

Dianne slipped into a coma and remained in it for fourteen days. Her father anointed her with oil and prayed, "Dear God, please do not let my daughter die." Gangrene set into her lower legs—from mid-calf down. While she was in the coma, the doctors had to amputate both legs at mid-calf. But God answered her father's prayer.

When I saw Dianne, I found my friend with no bitterness. She said to me, "When Ron wheeled me into the house in my wheelchair, I sat in front of the mirror and looked at my little body. When I finished my sob, I said, 'Okay, God, what is next?' and got on with my life."

When I said, "Dianne, they have ruined your life" (not very encouraging words, I admit), she answered, "Oh, Honey, we are 57, not 27. I have lived a full life." When I said, "Dianne, you will never dance with Ron again," she answered, "Oh, Honey, I got to walk in the desert with Ron and saw a desert tortoise and that was special." When I said, "But, Dianne, you are going to be walking on prosthetics for the rest of your life." she answered, "Oh, Honey, I have so much to live for. There are so many people I can encourage whose circumstances are worse than mine." When I swooped in with my killer-statement and said, "Are you going to sue them?" she answered, "Honey, people make mistakes. What is the point of suing?" (I have come to realize her use of the name Honey came after the amputation and is her way of saying how much she cares for people who are close to her.)

Later, I had the privilege of doing a radio interview with her via telephone to a station in Wisconsin. She said, "Every day when I wake up, it is my choice: 'Am I going to put on my grumpy face or ask God how He wants to use me today?' The choice is mine." She went on to say, "I do not believe God planned this for me but I do believe He can use it in my life and in the lives of others."

Dianne has testified before Congress and the Nevada State Legislature about malpractice caps. Indeed, the only time I have heard her be negative is when she told me about flying on the same plane with ten doctors from Las Vegas to Carson City, the capital of Nevada, to testify there. The doctors, who were wearing sports jackets/suits and dress shirts and ties on the plane, came into the hearing room wearing their hospital knee-length lab coats to protest Dianne's wearing a skirt that showed her prosthetics. She usually wears long billowing slacks that hide the prosthetics. When she started her testimony, their protest was to get up and walk out of the hearing room together. (Actually, the odds were not fair. It would have taken more than ten doctors to intimidate my friend.) She said to me, "Honey, (there is that beautiful word again) do you know any doctors who wear their lab coats outside the hospital?" I had to admit—except for the doctors in the hearing room in Carson City, I did not know of any.

I have asked Dianne's permission to tell her story and spoken about her in many places. I know it embarrasses her, but I always send her an email after I tell her story and say, "Dianne, they loved you in (name of city)." Many times, I have had people come up to thank me for telling her story of faith and encouragement and they tell me how her story has helped them.

I write of Dianne here for several reasons. One is that she is evidence that we encourage other people when we choose to bring God into the picture—regardless of our circumstances. Often, those who are discouraged assume that somehow God has left the scene, has no interest in their plight or cannot work in their lives in the future. As Dianne said to me one time, "I would not have chosen to lose my legs but I cannot deny that He has done some special things in my life because of losing them."

Secondly, there are people in our lives, both friends and strangers, who need a touch of encouragement. If we are focused only on our situation, we are not able to focus on how we might encourage others. As we mentioned earlier, the title of Dr. Jim Kok's book is profound: **90% of Helping Is Just Showing Up**. In a counseling class in seminary, we were told that most help is given, not by pastors or counselors, but by friends who simply tell the person who is discouraged that they love him.

Thirdly, I am learning from Dianne that, regardless of our situation, there is no reason to quit trusting in God and there is no reason to quit looking out for others. When Jesus said He came not to be served but to serve, He not only was explaining that His mission was to die for the sins of the world, but He was also encouraging us to have the same motivation in life.

Dianne wrote the following message at Christmas time:

I often wonder, when I really take a look at myself in the mirror, 'How can this change in me ever have led to such a rewarding life?' This period of reflection comes as I wheel by a full-length mirror in my dressing area off my bedroom. Good things often follow some of the largest challenges in our lives. I guess you ask, 'Dianne, are you crazy? I wouldn't want to face what you face every day of your life.' The truth is I wouldn't want you to face this every day. I love you too much. However, I have friends who survived their own crisis. I know how they did it ... they worked through some of the very worst of times and found the light at the end. Have a wonderful Christmas. Love to you all this Christmas.

Let me see ... what was it that had me so preoccupied that I could not take the time to think about or encourage my friend? I think you agree with me, Dianne Gobel Meyer is a remarkable and encouraging person.

Pianos Never Seemed the Same – Jim

I mentioned in Chapter 1 that during the trip John and I took to the Holy Land, I asked him why God doesn't just directly communicate to us. John responded, "He does, if you pay close enough attention." Little did John know how much encouragement and eternal value would come from his encouraging comment.

I have learned that there is chatter going on in our heads—without our permission—most of the time. If you are asking yourself right now, "What's he talking about? I don't have chatter going on in my head," that is the exact chatter I am talking about! The chatter is not the essence of you because you are separately aware of it as something going on that you are not directing. Sometimes our chatter is just meaningless daydreaming, distracting us from what should be our real focus.

But as John said to me in Israel, if we listen closely, God speaks to us—if we are not distracted by our chatter. Why do I believe it is God speaking? Because this inner voice usually asks of me what I am not naturally inclined to do.

Years ago, I was in my hometown and visited the church of my youth that I attended with my best friend, Jim Evans. I was surprised that, for a large church, it didn't have a grand piano. After the service, mostly out of curiosity, I approached the music director and inquired, "Why don't you have a grand piano?" He explained that the sound board in their old piano had cracked and they were short of funds to replace it.

Immediately, I felt down deeply that God was presenting an opportunity to me for giving to Him by providing a new piano. But I try not to make impulse decisions. During the week, I reflected upon what had happened. I continued to be moved by an inner voice that encouraged me to provide a piano. That inner voice would occasionally compete with my own selfish economic voice that would protest, "That's a lot of money, what are you thinking?"

The following week, my best friend Jim's mother, Ruth, died. She was a charter member of the church when it was founded fifty years earlier. She had a challenging life as a single mother and a first grade teacher. Her husband, Roy, died when Ruth was a young mother, and then she lost my friend, Jim, when he was eighteen and she was in her forties.

Ultimately, the inner voice prevailed, and I called Jane, Jim's surviving older sister and Ruth's only other child. I told her about the church piano and asked her permission to donate a piano in her mother's name as a founding member of the church. After listening, Jane remained quiet and then replied, "How strange. I had forgotten all about it until you just mentioned it, but when my father died, my mother received $10,000 from my father's life insurance policy. She used much of that to buy the church piano."

Amazing! Nearly fifty years earlier, Ruth felt moved to donate the church piano.

A spiritual rush went right through me. A coincidence? If you had lived my life—one that has been spiritually challenged in matters of faith—you would not think that. For me, with John's encouragement, I paid attention and responded. God responded in a compelling, beautiful way that catapulted my faith.

What an honor and joy it was to memorialize the sacrifice and spirituality of my best friend's mother by replacing the piano in the auditorium of the church we shared.

Giving Encouragement is a Strength, Not a Weakness – John

After I discovered drugs had invaded my family, I was devastated, as you can imagine. It was a Sunday afternoon and I was sitting in the den relaxing after a busy day at church. The phone rang and it was Rich Gunderson, a friend calling from Minnesota. He asked, "How are you?" I responded, "Do you know what happened?" because I assumed he had heard about the drug issue in our family. He did not know about it, and he was shocked. He said, "You have been on my mind, and I took that as a prompting from God to call you." I learned some lessons that day. Often, when someone is on our mind for a period of time, it is God's way of prompting us to contact them. I have started doing just that since my friend called sixteen years ago. I also learned that encouragement does not have to be something profound. It is often just a call, a note or an email to let someone know we care and we love him.

Not all encouragement comes unknowingly. When I was struggling to get my equilibrium after being hit by the ton of bricks over drugs in our family, a college friend, Keys Fort, called me at the office. He had heard about the problem. He asked if I knew his situation. I did not because we had not remained in close contact. He told me he was a recovering alcoholic and was living soberly one day at a time. He encouraged me that many people surmount the temptation to drink or use and that he was living proof of it. He gave me permission to call him any time. His call came at just the right time. His words were words that I needed to hear. Sadly, Keys died during open heart surgery before I could meet with him personally to thank him for his encouragement to me that day. I can only honor Keys' encouraging me by continuing to tell people how he helped at a crucial time in my life.

I am not sure macho men want to think about encouragement. But they are usually the ones who are hiding insecurities behind the macho persona. Plus, I do not think Jesus would qualify as a macho man in our society because He was honest, did not hide things and dealt with others with truth and grace. He lived His life with strength and faith; He did not have to broadcast it.

So in this whole discussion of encouragement, we must realize we men need to be willing to receive encouragement, and we need to be willing to give encouragement. Giving encouragement is not a sign of weakness but a sign of strength. And it is a sign of honesty. On a humorous note, I think of golfing with my friend, James Fillingame, who is a very good golfer. It was a par four hole, and it was my second shot. With tongue in cheek, I said, "James, this shot is for eagle," which meant I not only would get to the green but also would hole the shot—neither of which I could do. He said nothing, so I said, "Aren't you going to encourage me?" He looked at me and said, "Yes, I am going to encourage you not to lie to yourself." It was a funny moment but also a moment of reality: genuine encouragement is not fluff; it is telling the truth in a helpful way.

One of the most rewarding and humbling moments in life is when you have the sense God has used you in someone else's life. Sadly, over the years, I have missed many of the signals He has sent telling me to contact someone. There is no trouble with His communication skills; the trouble is with my spiritual antennae and my being more concerned about myself than others.

Recently, a friend in another state did not return a phone call. He did not answer an email...then a second email. Another phone call went unreturned. I knew he was not angry with me, as we had not seen each other for almost a year. I finally tracked him down and told him I was concerned about him. I asked if he was okay. He told me he had gone through some tough business challenges and family issues. I had no advice. I did not know what he was experiencing. I just listened. I knew of only two things to say: First, "I am so sorry." And second, "Though I know you do not know how it hurts to have a child addicted, neither do I know how much it hurts to experience what you are experiencing. But I care, and I will pray." That was a rewarding and humbling moment to be able to encourage my friend.

I have also learned that those in pain are often the best equipped to touch the lives of others who are hurting. With permission, I include this letter I wrote to a friend I met when we were seventeen years old. We were at a student council conference before our senior year of high school and later became fraternity brothers at the University of Oregon. I wrote this letter when his wife was very ill with cancer.

Dear Don:

I do not know if I told you that three weeks ago today I was in Cedar Rapids, Iowa, speaking at the funeral of one of my very good friends who was one of our board members of You're Not Alone. He came home from vacation in San Diego, slipped on the carpet, fell down the basement stairs, hit his head and suffered severe head trauma and died a few days later without ever regaining consciousness. He is greatly missed. His wife just sent me this note via email. I thought it might encourage you:

John, on my computer is this little note, "No winter lasts forever; no spring skips its turn." I am so blessed. Yes, I miss Dick, don't get me wrong. But he loved my joy and I want that joy to continue. Mary Jen

Don, again, I do not know how you feel. I am so sorry about this situation with your dear Linda. I cannot imagine what you feel. Your friend, John

High Performance friendships are mutually encouraging friendships.

Christ's Approach to Encouragement and Eternal Values

When Jesus was in the Upper Room in Jerusalem giving His men their final marching orders before He went out to be arrested and then crucified, He told them it was to their advantage that He go away. He promised He would send the Comforter (one of the names for the Holy Spirit) to them. The word comfort means to come along side and put your arm around someone in need. So Jesus was telling His friends He understood their need to be comforted. He was also saying that all His followers—subsequent to the eleven who were with Him that night in Jerusalem—would also need to be comforted.

When Jesus left the Upper Room, He went to the Garden of Gethsemane to pray before He was arrested. He had the three disciples with whom He was the closest, nearby to pray for Him and give Him encouragement. Sadly, they fell asleep and gave Him no comfort. If anything, they probably gave Him some discouragement. Finally, an angel ministered to Him. Regardless of the failure of His closest friends, we see Jesus in need of comfort and encouragement. It follows that if Jesus the God/man needed encouragement, we as human men need encouragement. The man who says he does not need encouragement from another is somehow saying he is better than Christ—who needed encouragement from others. We know there is no such man; we know he is not telling the truth. There is a need somewhere; it is what we keep hidden that keeps us sick and prevents Christ from healing that need.

Jesus said that on the ultimate judgment day the person who has given a cup of water to a small person in the kingdom of God will be rewarded. Jesus is elevating the value of serving and encouraging other people. Thus, we must make sure we are thinking as He was teaching us to think—and not as many macho men in our society who try to influence us by saying that real men do not encourage others.

The Apostle Paul gives us further understanding of what Jesus meant when He talked about the need for the Comforter and our need for comfort. The Apostle wrote that God gives us comfort in our time of need so that we are able to give comfort to others. It is a truism that the person who is most qualified to give us comfort is the person who has experienced the pain and discomfort we are experiencing. In this sense, Jesus does not waste our sorrows and pains but heals us if we allow Him to work in our lives. Then when we are healed He brings us into the lives of others to give them comfort just as He has comforted us.

In this chapter on encouragement, it seems the proper time to encourage ourselves as co-authors and you as the readers to take the next step with Christ. There is no one like Him in history. As C.S. Lewis said:

A man who was merely a man and said the sort of things Jesus said would not be a great moral teacher. He would either be a lunatic—on the level with a man who says he is a poached egg—or he would be the devil of hell. You must take your choice. Either this was, and is, the Son of God or else a madman or something worse. You can shut Him up for a fool, or you can fall at His feet and call Him Lord and God. But let us not come with any patronizing nonsense about His being a great human teacher. He has not left that open to us.

He has a claim on our lives. If you have not met Him, then this is a good time to do so. If you do not believe Christ is deity, this is a great time to examine the evidence for His statements, "If you have seen Me, you have seen the Father...the Father and I are one...I am the way, the truth and the life and no one comes to the Father except through Me." If you have met Him, this is a great time to consider the next piece of work He wants to do in your life to continue to conform you to His image.

Principles of Encouragement and Eternal Values

Words of encouragement do not have to be profound—just sincere. As John said earlier, when his father died, Jim's parent's sent a card that simply said, "We care." John has referred to that simple but profound message often in sermons around the world and how, like the widow's mite, so much was said with so little.

Words of encouragement work best when we do not try to sermonize but just communicate love and concern.

Men who cannot give encouragement are men who need to be touched by Jesus. Their lack of ability to encourage shows need for growth not strength.

Men who cannot admit they need encouragement are hiding a fear. Jesus knew we all need encouragement and, therefore, He sent the Comforter to us.

If we do not admit our humanity and our frailty, our friends cannot encourage us. It is what we fail to share with our friends that cannot be helped through high performance friendship.

Our children, when they are in pain, can reveal the need for comfort more than almost any other person or situation in our lives.

The principle message of Christ is encouraging and eternal.

We know we are incapable of living sin-free lives as Christ did; accordingly, we need forgiveness. Psychologists affirm the power of it. We, especially those who have behaved in terrible ways, need to believe we can be forgiven. Without the release of forgiveness, mental illness can result from overwhelming guilt. Consider Judas: after betraying Jesus, he felt so guilty he hung himself—yet Christ would have forgiven him as he did Paul for persecuting Christians.

Psychologists also affirm that the act of forgiving is much healthier than harboring resentment. Fifty percent of mental hospital beds are filled with people who are angry. Alcoholics Anonymous has research that tells us that a high percentage of alcoholics struggle with anger.

Christ gave His life so we can completely and forever be forgiven. All we have to do to accept this amazing grace is believe in Him and ask for forgiveness for our sinfulness. Be comforted; we don't actually have to remember each and every sin for it to be forgiven—none of us can remember them all. We just don't want to deny the ones we are aware of, including those that a good friend might call to our attention.

When we acknowledge our sins to God and commit to change, we are complete with Him because He forgives perfectly, which includes both forgiving and forgetting. In our imperfect forgiving, we are more inclined to never let others forget that we forgave.

Striving to be Christ-like in our forgiveness is a most worthy goal. Jim and his father-in-law, Kent, have had only one disagreement, pertaining to raising children. It was years ago. They both apologized but Jim acknowledges he failed to forget. Several years later, as he became wiser, Jim mentioned to Kent that he now agreed with his point of view. Kent looked at Jim with a kind but blank look and said, "I don't remember this disagreement." At first, Jim thought he was kidding. He wasn't. Jim tried to refresh his memory, but Kent responded in a gentle manner that revealed he not only didn't remember but preferred not to do so. It no longer mattered to him. In a Christ-like fashion, he forgave and forgot. Jim often says that Kent is among his friends who teach him by example how to be more Christ-like.

Being forgiven and being forgiving does wonders for our mental well being—forgiveness for health. Living our lives under grace encourages us to live Christ-like lives, not out of fear of punishment but out of inspiration from gratitude.

After believing and accepting forgiveness, we are to follow the great commandment—love one another as God loves us.

What a simple, beautiful way to live—believe and love.

Would the world and friendships not be transformed if we all did?

Discussion Questions and Applications

1. Can you think of a time when someone brought great encouragement to your life? How did they do it?

2. Can you think of a time when you brought great encouragement to someone else? How did you do it?

3. Why is it that so many men cannot admit the need for encouragement?

4. What do we learn about encouragement from Dianne Gobel Meyer's experience of losing her legs and her response to this tragedy?

5. What do we learn from Christ sending us the Comforter, the Holy Spirit?

6. What do we learn about encouragement from what Christ experienced in the Garden of Gethsemane?

7. Is there someone in your life to whom you should give encouragement in the near future?

8. How can we encourage ourselves to take the next step with Christ?

9. In what ways would our friendships become high performance if we believed and loved?

10. What stories of encouragement and eternal values can you share in a helpful manner with your friends?

Summary and Conclusion

As we were writing this book and sharing it with friends, they gave us much encouragement for writing a book about men and friendship. The affirming response was High Performance Friendships when achieved are indeed a wonderful *Win/Win* phenomenon. But one question came up often: "How does your book help the man who doesn't have high performance friends or know how to make them?"

We decided to address that issue in the Summary and Conclusion.

Mirror, Mirror

We spoke in Chapter 9 about how relationships are like a mirror. The text stated:

Have you ever noticed how friendship can work like a mirror? When we are kind and thoughtful to others, we tend to stimulate those responses from others. And if we are selfish and thoughtless, we stimulate those responses from others.

Though we were speaking of kindness, the phenomenon of mirroring applies to our interaction with others in general. The biggest mistake we make is that we try to drive relationships rather than letting them evolve. If, for example, we want someone to be interested in us, we make the mistake of trying to be interesting so as to attract interest. What we should do is show interest in the other person and allow him to mirror that behavior back and become interested in us. If he doesn't respond by showing interest, does he really show friendship potential?

Here is where women have a major advantage over men. Women seem to intuitively know that to impress guys, they can just show interest and be impressed. They realize that by asking questions that allow guys to talk and brag, the guys think the women are fascinating.

We have observed one-sided conversations where a guy dominates a conversation with a woman who pays attention to a topic in which she is obviously not interested, e.g., an old truck he is customizing. When the less-than-interesting conversation ends, the man often compliments her on how interesting she is. In reality, because of the egocentricity of males, she was interesting simply because she showed interest in him and his interests!

Thus, we are suggesting that when we as men follow the mirroring principle, as well as learn from women who tend to be better conversationalists than men, we endeavor to be truly interested in the man to whom we are talking. Jesus said it is better to give than to receive. We men can learn to give by listening more and talking less. Most men are not as interested in a discussion of our successes as we think they are.

Five Levels of Friendship

In the spirit of Mirror, Mirror, it is important that we consider five levels of friendship that help us understand what we are projecting to our friends. As we said earlier, men often use the word friend, but there are different meanings for the word as described below. We must know what we want to achieve in our friendships. The choice is ours.

Level 5 – *Acquaintance*. This is a person whom we really do not know beyond a shallow "Hello, how are you?" But we have said it so often and so long, we refer to the person as a friend.

Level 4 – *Pal*. This is a person we know and with whom we do things, but we do not share and there is no great love or intimacy.

Level 3 – **Companion**. In companionship, there is genuine liking for each other; we enjoy being with one another and have similar interests. This level is characterized by Shared Activity. But discussions rarely show any vulnerability, and fears are not shared very often, if at all. Companions avoid conflict and challenge at all costs. Rarely is anything shared that produces character growth.

Level 2 – **Genuine Friendships**. In these relationships, there is a deep affection for one another and a deep commitment to each other. These friendships can be Christian, but they do not have to be. Men at this level are not afraid to say that they love one another. They strive to help each other grow.

Level 1 – **High Performance Friendships**. Knowing Christ and becoming conformed to His image is life's highest calling and ambition. Therefore, we conclude that the highest form of friendship is on a spiritual plane that transcends our physical, intellectual and spiritual lives. Thus, the friend who would help us grow spiritually and into closer conformity to Christ is the most intimate and important friend. It is at this level that we share most deeply, most intimately, and in a way that challenges both sides of the friendship. These friendships are characterized as transparent and selfless.

CHRISTLIKE Approach to Building Friendships

With this simple understanding of mirroring and the levels of friendship, we can now summarize the learning provided in each of the CHRISTLIKE chapters.

CHOOSING FRIENDS – If we are interested in someone as a potential friend, does it make sense to simply show interest in him by asking questions about his career, education, hobbies, cars, faith, etc.? Does this show interest and help us learn if there is a good match of interests for pursuing a friendship? This approach should motivate us to choose our friends wisely.

HUMILITY AND HONESTY – Are we drawn to people who are humble and honest? First, by showing interest and asking questions of others, are we demonstrating humility? Is it better not to speak of ourselves until we are asked? Are we more impressed with people who are honest, including making self-effacing, even humorous comments about their own short-comings? John once asked Jim if he was any good at basketball. Jim responded that he broke his wrist shooting baskets by himself (true story). When John asked how, Jim responded, "It was a personal foul." John laughed and sized up Jim as someone with humility, honesty and humor.

RESPECT – Are we more likely to receive respect by asking for it or by showing it?

INTIMACY – Are people more likely to share intimate thoughts and feelings with us if we are the first to share? However, if our sharing seems to make a potential friend uncomfortable, we are alerted that deep friendship may not be possible with that person. Or worse, if they gossip with what we share, that is a serious alert.

SUPPORT – This one is straightforward from the lessons we learn from Christ. He often made the first gesture of support, such as healing the sick, washing His disciples' feet or welcoming the social outcasts. These demonstrations of support not only expressed His love and friendship worthiness, but also created responsiveness to His teachings.

TEACH AND TRUST – If someone wants to learn, do you think teaching is a wonderful gesture of friendship? How can we best make it safe for someone to learn? Do we make it safe by never belittling someone for something they don't know? Do we make it safe for them and, even better, show humility and admiration by asking someone to teach us? Is that a collaborative way to build trust?

LOVE AND LOYALTY – Are love and loyalty best received when offered first? Puppies are quite instructive in this matter, supporting the adage that a dog is man's best friend. Have you noticed how an eager puppy wagging its tail enthusiastically is hard to resist? We know of people who claimed they would never have a dog being won over in a matter of minutes by the emotions even a puppy knows how to express. Of course, we have no tail to wag, but we can give an enthusiastic look of admiration, followed with a simple, "You are a good man who deserves the appreciation and loyalty he receives." Does that effectively make the point and provide support for friendship?

INDEPENDENCE AND INNER COMPASS – Do we find men more appealing when they project a sense of relaxed confidence and independence? Are we unimpressed by those who agree with whichever way the wind seems to be blowing and demonstrate no sense of right and wrong? Jim mentioned how easily one's credibility can be destroyed by a simple, dishonest gesture. As an example, Jim said, "John, as well as we know each other, do you realize that if a tip were left on a table when we sat down to lunch, and I put it in my pocket, you would have a hard time trusting me going forward." John smiled and replied, "You know, of course, that I would not allow you to take it."

KINDNESS – The chapter on kindness is where we introduced the concept of mirroring in relationships. Kindness begets kindness. Is there any better way to express friendship or interest in friendship than an unsolicited act of kindness? A selfless act?

ENCOURAGEMENT AND ETERNAL VALUES – This is one of the most under-utilized yet powerful ways to build friendships. It takes little effort to be thoughtful and to express a few words to encourage and provide an eternal perspective. When friends do that for us, besides the direct benefit, does it strengthen the bond of friendship?

In summary, perhaps the best endorsement we can provide for the CHRISTLIKE framework is that we developed further as friends as we worked together; we finished the book as even higher performance friends than when we started it.

Our Beliefs

Though we have expressed our faith throughout the book, as final thoughts, we would like to share our belief system. Prior to doing so, we acknowledge our rebellion and lack of faith—we resisted God for way too long. We are both sinners, and without forgiveness, we are not worthy to approach God when we die.

Jesus Christ, the Son of God, died on the cross to pay the price for our sinfulness. The resurrection of Jesus Christ is a historically validated event, and it is on that event that we base our faith in Jesus Christ as the Savior of the world through grace.

Christ gave His life so that we can completely and forever be forgiven—past, present and future. It is our choice to accept or reject this gift of amazing grace.

In receiving Christ, we ask for forgiveness for our sinfulness and ask Christ to enter our lives. This is a spiritual birth that begins an amazing relationship with Christ, God and the Holy Spirit. It can be achieved by a simple prayer of expressing one's sinfulness and imperfection, asking Christ to forgive that sinfulness and inviting Him into our life.

Living under grace inspires us to honor God by conforming to the image of Christ through the empowerment of the Holy Spirit. We find sin less appealing because it is in conflict with our new spiritual selves.

Nonetheless, we are human, and we still fail and sin. When we do, even though we are already forgiven, we need to confess (agree with God) our sins and turn from them.

After believing in Christ and accepting His forgiveness, we are to follow the great commandment: Love one another as God loves us.

Epilogue

A Tribute To Our Fathers As Friends

We both had the good fortune of having fathers who, as we became adults, were also good friends. Both of our fathers provided fundamental male relationships. As we conclude the book, we would like to share tribute to each of them using the words John wrote to his church three years after his father died and the words Jim shared at his father's memorial service.

To Harry Vawter – John

He was a great man...great guy...a great father. He said while visiting me three years before he died that he no longer viewed my brother and me as sons but as friends. What a thrill to have that type of relationship. I really miss my father...and my friend.

And yet, his departure has allowed me to be honest with some truth that I had avoided for a long time. My father was a battered child... and a poor child. One year, he and two brothers rotated the use of two sets of clothes by staying home from school every third day. One year, he did not go out for track even though he was favored to be the state champion in the half mile because he had no underwear and was too embarrassed to undress in the locker room. Early adulthood was no better.

I never knew why he did not want me to ride the rails home from college...a distance of 110 miles...with the other guys who did it for fun until he finally said, "I rode the rails west to avoid poverty, and to have you riding the rails for fun is more than I can handle." Somehow, all of this negative history seemed to put a cap on his emotional expressions and his being in touch with his feelings. He told me one time that the pain of being poor was so intense that he played the tough guy role to cover up his deep feelings of inferiority. He was so concerned never to be out of control because of his father's lack of control that he seldom expressed anger...or love. Those were emotions to keep in check. It was only later in life that he learned to express himself.

He was also unable to express pride in his accomplishments. Although my brother, sister and I have a total of eight earned degrees beyond high school...and although my father died as a successful businessman...he could not accept the fact that he had been a successful father or a successful businessman. When complimented for his accomplishments, he would always respond, "You do what you have to do."

He was a product of that so pervasive, but so wrong, philosophy in our society that says fathers hug their daughters but never their sons. It was not until the latter years of his life that my father began to feel comfortable hugging my brother and me. In his book, **Men: A Book for Women**, Jim Wagenvoord describes this philosophy: "To be a man, a real man, we tend to believe that:

- He shall not cry.
- He shall not display weakness.
- He shall not need affection, gentleness or warmth.
- He shall comfort but not desire comforting.
- He shall be needed but not need.
- He shall touch but not be touched.
- He shall be steel but not flesh.
- He shall be inviolate in his manhood.
- He shall stand alone."

Unfortunately, I picked up on that philosophy. I thought tough guys did not cry, so I made certain never to do that. I was careful never to appreciate people for making an impact on my life. People told me I was hard to get to know, and that was just the way I liked it. Only my wife knew the real me.

And then my father died very suddenly following surgery for a brain tumor. At the funeral, I watched his friends hugging, crying and comforting. I heard people tell how much he had meant to them: a timely loan, a kind word, a helpful gesture. I heard them tell how much they would miss him. All of a sudden, I realized I was the loser for keeping people away from me. And so I admitted why I was closed and began to open up. It's a whole new wonderful world.

As I reflect on my relationship with my father-friend, I wish I had said, "I love you" more often; I wish we had embraced more; I wish I had not felt embarrassed kissing his cheek when he lay in the hospital dying of the brain tumor; I wish I had taken him out to lunch more often when, after marrying and having children, I moved back to my hometown for six years (even though he never would let me pay); and I wish I had phoned him more and made him talk (even though he did not like to talk on the telephone) after I moved to Minneapolis. I wish a lot of things...but you can't go back when your father is dead.

But I have a son, and I can love and hug him. And I have a brother, and I am learning to hug him. And I have the people in my church, and although I may feel uncomfortable hugging them, I can begin to try, and I can encourage them to express their love to their children, parents or loved ones. Many are locked up inside themselves, as my father was in so many ways, and as I guess I am in some ways. Since we are still living, we can let God break those chains that prevent us from saying, "I love you," from hugging and from letting people for whom we care know that we care. Letting God break these chains conforms us to the image of Christ.

Today's a great day to start...so let's hug our sons...hug our daughters...hug our brothers...hug our fathers...hug our sisters...hug someone...hug me. It is true; we are here to love—and to show it. Let's begin loving and expressing it.

To Mead Wetherbe – Jim

My father, like John's, had a difficult childhood. The second of eleven children, his father (my grandfather) died unexpectedly when my father was in the eighth grade. He and his older brother had to drop out of school and work to support the family. He went back to high school at age 21 and still managed to graduate from college with a degree in physics.

Not having a normal childhood that involved fun and sports, my father lacked most of the skills a father would have to pass on to his son. To get transportation, he had to buy a broken down old car and learn how to overhaul the engine. He shared that skill with me as a teenager when I purchased a run-down 1950 Studebaker, and we overhauled the engine together. He did the same with my two older brothers, Bond and Joe.

He had a distinguished career as a computer scientist and computer programmer. He worked on the hydrogen bomb and wrote much of the software to support the space program. And he did help me learn how to program computers back when the skill was rare. It launched my career in information systems. I dedicated the first book I wrote on systems design to him with the words: "In a field as new as information systems, few of us can say 'my old man was in the business.' I dedicate this book to my father Mead Bond Wetherbe Sr."

My father was a man of great faith, which included a scientific assessment of his reasons.

I once asked him how he shared his faith without being offensive or repellent. He responded, "I have learned the best way is to set an example with the way you live that prompts curiosity in others. If others ask how I approach my life, that is when I share my faith."

My father did set a good example. I remember once on a trip, my mother accidentally left her purse at a restaurant. She didn't discover the mistake until an hour and sixty miles later, which required a two hour round trip to remedy. She was so furious with herself she was openly self- critical for miles. My father, who was driving, finally reached over and placed his hand gently on her leg and kindly said, "I forgave you miles ago; can you forgive yourself?"

It is interesting how we often define others by the stories we can tell about them. Here is another. When I was a teenager, I backed my car out of the garage into my father's car. My father took as much pride as anyone in his vehicles. I remember the sick feeling I felt as I got out and looked at the damage on his car but the lack of it on mine. For a moment, the temptation to drive off and deny knowing anything raced through my mind. But I decided to face the music. I have never forgotten my father's kind, understanding response when I went back in the house and shared the bad news. He knew how badly I felt and suppressed whatever anger he might have felt. He was so Christ-like in that moment.

His examples of forgiveness were powerful examples that carried forward in my life with my six children—especially when they became teenage drivers. As they had their auto mishaps, my father's example enhanced my ability to get a grace-grant from God when needed. As I had done, one of my children backed into another car in the driveway—on two separate occasions! As an extraordinary grace test, the second time involved my hour-old new sports car that she had previously parked in the driveway after a quick test drive.

At my father's memorial service, as the professional speaker, I was asked to share some thoughts including the ones above. I was happy and confident to do it. That day, I learned about the throat god who can create a lump so big in your throat you can barely speak. Due to the unrestrained crying it was not my best delivery—but no one questioned my sincerity.

During the next decade, my mother passed away. Bond, my oldest brother and a high performance friend, offered to speak at the memorial. I warned him about the throat god, but as a professor and consultant, he was as confident as I was at our father's memorial service. He was not concerned, explaining that this was a celebration of our Mother's life and that he fully intended to make it upbeat and uplifting. He started so cheerfully, "Welcome, we are here today to celebrate Marguerite Wetherbe's life…" And just like that the throat god took him out—like he had done to me.

We teased each other about the phenomenon and took pride in the fact that the throat god expressed our emotions for both of our wonderful parents.

I admire John's ability to speak so soundly when he is called upon to provide eulogies for those he has loved and lost.

References

Barnard, Chester, **Functions of the Executive**, Harvard Press 1938 and 1968

Campbell, Donavon, **Joker One: A Marine Platoon's Story of Courage, Leadership, and Brotherhood**, Random House 2009

Farley, Andrew, **The Naked Gospel**, Zondervan 2009

Fasteau, **The Male Machine**, McGraw Hill 1980

Feinstein, John, **Moment of Glory: The Year Underdogs Ruled Golf**, Back Bay Books 2010

Greenleaf, Robert, **Servant Leaders**, Paulist Press 1977, 1991 and 2002

Holman Bible Dictionary 1991

Kimmel, Michael, **Manhood in America**, Second Edition, Oxford University Press 2005

Kimmel, Michael, **Guyland: The Perilous World Where Boys Become Men**, HarperCollins 2008

Kok, James R., **90% of Caring is Just Showing Up**, CRC Publications 2007

Lewis, C. S., **Mere Christianity Harper** 1952, renewed 1980

McDowell, Josh, **More than a Carpenter**, Wheaton Books 1977

McGill, **The McGill Report on Male Intimacy**, Harpercollins 1986

Miller, **Men and Friendship**, Tarcher 1991

Nygaard, Reuel, **From Tragedy to Triumph**, Cook Publishing 1994

Pheffer, Jeffrey, **"How Economic Language and Assumptions Undermine Ethics: Rediscovering Human Values"**, Inaugural Presentation, Escola Chair of Ethics 2004

Robertson, A. T., **Word Pictures in the New Testament**, Broadman Press 1930

Rotundo, Anthony, **American Manhood**, Basic Books 1993

Smith, David, **The Friendless American Male**, Regal Books 1983

Tournier, Paul, **Secrets**, John Knox Press 1965

Vawter, John, **Hit by a Ton of Bricks**, Westbow 2011

Vawter, John, **Uncommon Graces**, Navpress 1998

Vines, Thom with John Michael Vesta, **Tragedy & Trust**, Authorhouse 2011

Wagenvoord, Jim, **Men: A Book for Women**, Avon Publishers 1978

Wetherbe, James, **Faith Logic**, Mead Publishing 2007

Wetherbe, James and Bond Wetherbe, **So, What's Your Point?**, 4th Edition, Mead Publishing 2012

Yoder, Wes, **Bond of Brothers**, Zondervan 2010

Young, William, **The Shack**, Windblown Media 2007

Index of Bible Verses

INTRODUCTION

Matthew 18:15	Going to your brother in private
John 1:14	Grace and truth
Luke 6:31	Do unto others
Matthew 26:74-75	Peter denied Christ
1 John 1:1-7	Walking as Jesus walked on earth

CHAPTER ONE – Choose Friends Wisely

Page 31

John 1:14	Grace and truth

Page 32

Matthew 13:3	Parable of sower
Luke 6:31	Golden Rule

Page 33

Philippians 2:6-8	Jesus did not consider equality
Philippians 2:3	Consider others better than you
Proverbs 1:10	Do not let sinners entice you
Hebrews 10:24-25	Consider how to stimulate

Page 34

Proverbs 22:24-25	Avoid hot tempered man
Proverbs 22:24-25	You can learn ways of easily angered man
Proverbs 1:10	Do not be enticed
Proverbs 13:20	Walk with wise men
Proverbs 16:28	Perverse man

Page 35
John 13:27   Judas, do what you will do

Page 36
Mark 4:23   He who has ears

CHAPTER TWO – Humility and Honesty

Page 54
John 4:34   My sustenance is will
John 17:4   I have accomplished
Luke 19:11   Talents
Ephesians 4:11   Jesus' gifted people
1 Corinthians 4:7   What are you so puffed up about?

Page 55
Matthew 11:29   Gentle and humble of heart
Galatians 5:22-23   Fruit of the Spirit
John 16:7   I will send the Spirit

Page 56
Matthew 7:4   Log out of your eye
Galatians 5:22-23   Gentleness and patience

Page 59
Proverbs 27:2   Lips of another praise you
Matthew 27:11   It is as you say

Page 60
John 17:4   I have accomplished

CHAPTER THREE – Respect

Page 69
1 Timothy 5:2   Do not look down on youth
1 Timothy 5:1   treat an older man with respect

Page 71
John 14:6   I am the way, truth and life

Page 73
John 20:27   Put your hands in My side
John 1:14   Grace and truth
John 3:34-35   Nicodemus

Page 74
John 3:1-15   Being reborn
Romans 5:8   While we were yet sinners
Romans 5:10   Enemies of God
James 1:19   Listen first

Page 75
Luke 6:31   Golden Rule
Matthew 22:39   Love your neighbor as self

CHAPTER FOUR – Intimacy

Page 89
John 11:35   Lazarus
Matthew 26:36-46   Gethsemane

CHAPTER FIVE – Support

Page 99
1 Timothy 6:11   Flee temptation

Page 107
Luke 5:16   Jesus went alone to pray
John 16:7   I will send Comforter

Page 108
James 2:1-4   Bless you...be fed and warm
Matthew 26:36-46   Overwhelmed...fell asleep
Philippians 2:6-8   Even unto death

Page 109

Luke 23:39-41	Thieves on cross
Exodus 20:5, Psalm 100:2	Worship jealousy
Acts 13:2	Minister to God
John 19:26	Behold your son
Proverbs 17:17, 18:24	Friends
Hebrews 10:24-25	Stimulate one another

Page 110

1 Peter 3:18	Jesus forgave our sin
Psalm 103:12	Our sin is gone

Page 111

1 John 4:8	Perfect love casts out fear

CHAPTER SIX – Trust and Teach

Page 121

Ephesians 5:18	Drunkenness is wrong

Page 124

John 1:14	Grace and truth

Page 125

Colossians 4:6	Season speech with grace
Matthew 5:37	Let yes be yes
Matthew 9:12	Jesus answered Pharisees
Proverbs 18:17	Hear both sides of an argument
Mark 10:45	Jesus came to serve, not be served

Page 126

Matthew 16:23	Get behind Me, Satan
Matthew 20:20-23	James and John sitting in heaven's best seat
John 13:8	Peter wash feet
John 18:17	Peter denied Christ three times

CHAPTER SEVEN – Love and Loyalty

Page 143
John 13:34-35   Love shows discipleship
Matthew 22:39   Love your neighbor

Page 144
Luke 10:25-37   Good Samaritan
Galatians 5:22-23   Fruit of Spirit—faithfulness
Proverbs 18:24   Won't carry load and closer than a
                            brother
Proverbs 20:6   Hard to find faithful friend
Proverbs 27:5-7   Open rebuke better than hidden love

Page 145
Proverbs 27:17   Iron sharpens iron
Proverbs 27:6   The kisses of an enemy
Romans 2:11   No partiality
Matthew 27:46   My God, My God
John 18:17   Peter denies three times
Ephesians 4:32   Forgive as God did in Christ

Page 146
Acts 20:35   It is better to give

CHAPTER EIGHT – Independence and Inner Compass

Page 151
Romans 1:20   Since creation
Jeremiah 29:13   Seek Me and find Me

Page 156
Ephesians 4:28   Stealing
Matthew 7:4   Log and speck
John 8:7   He who is without sin

Page 163

John 14:6 Way, truth and life

John 4:34 His will is my sustenance

Page 164

2 Corinthians 10:5 Obedience

Matthew 5:3 Poor in spirit

Matthew 5:3 Poor in spirit/spiritually destitute

Page 165

John 15:5 Apart from Me

John 14:6 Way, truth, life

Page 167

Hebrews 12:6 Those whom He loves

CHAPTER NINE – Kindness

Page 182

John 15:13 No greater love

Page 184

Isaiah 53:3 Man of sorrows

Page 185

Luke 23:34 Father forgive

Luke 23:39-43 Thieves

John 19:27 Your mother

Luke 7:38 Woman with hair

John 14:6 Way, truth and life

Proverbs 11:25-26 Helping others

Page 186

John 8:1-11 Woman caught in adultery

Luke 17:11-19 Ten lepers

Mark 5:24-34 Woman with issue of blood

John 1:14 Grace and truth

Galatians 5:22-23 Fruit of Spirit

Page 187
John 15:5   Apart from Me you can do nothing

CHAPTER TEN – Encouragement and Eternal Values

Page 195
Mark 10:45   Jesus did not come to be served

Page 199
John 1:14   Grace and truth

Page 201
John 16:7   Comforter will be sent
Luke 23:39-46   Jesus praying in Gethsemane

Page 202
Mark 9:24   Giving a cup of water
2 Corinthians 1:4   Comforting others
John 14:9   If you have seen me
John 10:13   The Father and I are one
John 14:6   I am the way, truth and life